# SELLING YOUR CRAFTS

# SELLING YOUR CRAFTS

## NORBERT N. NELSON

Published in cooperation with
The American Craftsmen's Council

 VAN NOSTRAND REINHOLD COMPANY
NEW YORK   CINCINNATI   TORONTO   LONDON   MELBOURNE

Van Nostrand Reinhold Company Regional Offices:
New York   Cincinnati   Chicago   Millbrae   Dallas

Van Nostrand Reinhold Company International Offices:
London      Toronto      Melbourne

Copyright © 1967 by Litton Educational Publishing, Inc.
Library of Congress Catalog Card Number 67-24697
ISBN 0-442-25946-8

Published by Van Nostrand Reinhold Company
450 West 33rd Street, New York, N.Y. 10001

Published simultaneously in Canada by
Van Nostrand Reinhold Limited

16   15   14   13   12   11   10   9   8   7   6   5   4   3

# Acknowledgments

The existence of this volume is a direct result of the interest of the American Craftsmen's Council, and most specifically of Miss Lois Moran of that organization. It is hoped that this book will satisfy the need they expressed for a clear and simple guide to assist new craftsmen to enter the marketplace successfully and small craftsmen to grow into larger producers.

I cannot overestimate the value of the counsel given me by Mrs. Rose Slivka and her staff at *Craft Horizons* during the decade past. Parts of this work previously appeared as articles in their publication and their readers' reactions to the published material have helped to shape the content of this text.

Obviously, I could not have written such a book at all without the cooperation given me by the craftsmen, craft merchants, legal counsel and other specialists mentioned herein. Their interest and cooperation has provided the substance of this work.

I must acknowledge a debt of gratitude to Mr. Irving Richards and the late George Cooper of Richards Morgenthau Company and other members of their organization extraordinary, under whose patient tutelage I spent a decade learning my "trade." The multitudinous clients, manufacturers, buyers, salesmen and co-workers with whom I have had the pleasure of working during the past eighteen years have all made a significant contribution to the theories and practice contained herein, for it is they who shaped and continue to shape the world of the marketplace with which this book is concerned.

# Preface

In the face of advanced industrialization there has sprung up in America a thriving creative craftsmanship. A combination of excellent educational facilities and instruction plus a growing and affluent audience has encouraged the development of many skilled American craftsmen. Their work, while obviously of limited production in a technological society, nevertheless has an important role to play in the marketplace.

Man's need and desire for individual expression lead him to seek out objects for his environment which delight and serve him; that the most unique of these objects originate from the hands of skilled craftsmen is true of the present as it is of the past. And so the task for the producing craftsman is not just designing and making his craft but bringing it to a buying public as well.

How to sell his product is a major consideration for any person who wishes to sustain himself as a producing craftsman. Whether his craft is his sole source of income or only a supplement does not alter the need for basic marketing knowledge and approach. Such knowledge is by no means corruptive of creativity but rather a liberating force. It is more often the craftsman who lacks or eschews a businesslike approach who is deprived of the full enjoyment that his craft can bring him.

Up to now little has been written on the subject of marketing crafts and certainly in no single volume such as this have so many aspects of marketing crafts been discussed. Thus the publication of Norbert Nelson's text is an important contribution. In light of his excellent background in marketing and his realistic attitude and understanding of the craftsman's position in twentieth-century America, it is particularly fortunate that Mr. Nelson has had the opportunity of sharing his thoughts in this book. It remains for the reader to use these thoughts in a way appropriate to his own work. Just as there is great variety of artistic expression, so too are there varied ways of merchandising.

The author remarks in his second chapter that the craftsman's success in the marketplace may well rest principally on his talent as a designer. Surely there is no more important responsibility for today's craftsman than that he continually grow in design ability. His inventiveness and individuality must always be expressed or he will forfeit the very basis upon which his present status rests.

Lois Moran
Director, Regional Program
American Craftsmen's Council

# Introduction

Marketing is one of those modern terms which has become so common and varied in business usage that it has become unintelligible to the uninitiated. The confusion of its meaning is probably due in part to a Madisonavenuesque clique which has tried to make it into a mystique. In fact, and especially as applied to the crafts and other limited production industries, it means nothing more than the coordinated use of the various techniques of modern selling. The methods of converting merchandise into money in order to finance the production of more merchandise are simple to understand. Given a salable product and the willingness to engage in some trial and error efforts, you can build the basis of a successful business.

This text treats four basic information areas, giving you guidelines to assist your start in business: first, some basic facts about the unique market for handcrafts to help you observe more astutely and facilitate your own evaluations in the market; second, basic guidelines are included to help you prepare both your product and your production facility for this market; third, sales tools which will enable you to enter the marketplace successfully are discussed at length; finally, I have included concrete guidelines for beginning sales activity in various ways. If there were a simple fool-proof way to create products and sell them to capacity, the business world would be an easy place indeed in which to make a living. Unfortunately, as it is too frequently demonstrated, marketing is as much an art as a science. There are ground rules to be followed which will save many a false turn. However, beyond the application of these ground rules, each new entry of a product into the marketplace is an adventure.

Intuition is an important part of any marketer's equipment, especially in the category of highly designed style products into which most craft production falls. It can be developed with exposure and repeated efforts to sell. Mistakes are, or should be, an expected part of any new human endeavor, and the most you can hope to do is to minimize your mistakes, to keep them from being costly, and to learn from them. This book provides a framework within which to begin.

As an art, marketing calls on your imagination as much as does product development. Caution dictates that you do not break the rules until you know what they are and why they exist. Innovations are the lifeblood of the marketing adventure. Were it not for marketing innovations in recent years, there would be no supermarkets; you would still be paying a "momma and papa store" much higher prices for food. There would be no coin vending machines or drive-in movies, and all cars, like the Model-T, would be available in black. In most instances the world's most successful product group, especially if it is new, is likely to die on the vine if not imaginatively and effectively merchandised. Product development, without creative marketing, is likely to be as useless as a marketing effort without an adequate product.

The craftsman, the craft innovator at his best, has an obligation at this time. It is an obligation which can be effectively discharged only through exploitation of the market. That obligation is to bring, and keep bringing, to a world which is supplied with uniform products manufactured by large production complexes, products which do not contribute to the sameness of the world's goods. It is an important part of the craftsman's job to keep before the consuming public the spirit of uniqueness, beauty, and above all, the human qualities which characterize craft products. The fact that the craftsman or small industrial producer makes superior products is not enough. He must put his work where the world can see it, own it, use it and learn to love it. Only in this way can it actually influence the taste and upgrade the standards of the purchasing public at large.

The first time the potter sits down at his wheel, the wood turner at his lathe, or the weaver at his loom, innovation is not either expected or likely. Even a Picasso had some classical learning and basic experimentation to do. Thus it is in beginning to sell. The master salesman, like the master jeweler, is a joy to watch in action. He is a professional, having learned his trade through long years of work, exposure and educative errors. As in all things, some are better than others and not every salesman has the talent —and a talent it is—to be a master marketing man. He would never have found out if he is just adequate or actually superb, however, if he had never committed himself to trying. If a man on the street were to pick up a glass blower's pipe, draw material from the pot and begin to blow a vase, the chances are almost certain that he would fail on his first attempt. Starting to sell is easier than that because all of us have at one time or another done some selling and have watched others do it. So it is possible that on your very first try you will meet with success. If you don't, all you can do is what you did in your craft: try to figure out what went wrong and try again. Unless you are totally inarticulate about the thing you know best—your product—you will quickly start meeting with some success.

It is not the intention of this book to turn each craftsman into a skilled salesman. However, if you are going to use marketing techniques, it is well to know how they are used so that you can, very soon, make intelligent choices of the approaches, people, and systems you will use in your selling, and be competent to guide, motivate and coordinate them wisely.

The easiest way for most people to learn something is to become involved in it. After some exposure to marketing, an effort to sell, and some analysis of what you have done, you should develop into your own best salesman. After all, nobody knows more about your product than you do and nobody will be as concerned with its sale as you are. Motivation and knowledge are two basic qualifications for moving anything into the marketplace. If any sales manager, selling any product, were to lay down for his salesmen a series of basic prerequisites to selling, they might run something like this:

1. Know what you are selling. Know as much as you can about the product, its qualities (esthetic as well as physical), and how it is made and will perform. Certainly, know more than your customer is likely to know.
2. Know your competition. In brief, know how your product stacks up against competitive products which are also bidding for the consumer's dollars—often in the same place at the same time.
3. Learn what motivates your customer, either the retailer or the consumer, to purchase your product and others like it: prestige? profit? traffic-building excitement? When you think you know, use the features of your product which interest him to influence him to buy.
4. Be prepared to repeat your efforts. No salesman is 100% successful. Not every customer is right for any product. Effort stands above all the "tricks" of any trade, and only through repeated and sustained effort will success be achieved and maintained. Selling is work!

Most creative craftsmen are sensitive people. Their sensitivity has been developed toward the end of evaluating and analyzing things. It will also develop toward probing people and their motivations. With a sustained interest in selling—and it can be interesting—you will develop a sense about the marketability of your own wares and the reactions of the people who buy them. Once you have done so, the business of crafts will become doubly exciting.

One final ghost should be laid to rest before we proceed to the particulars at hand. The cry of commercialism has been leveled at the market by craftsmen. If commercialism means the successful exchange of the products of your hands and mind for money to create still more products, then indeed this book is preaching commercialism. If you accept the fact that you must continue to sell so that you can continue to produce, then you might as well learn to sell successfully. If, as these critics often erroneously suppose, competition means somehow down-styling your product to a "commercial level," whatever that is, then they will find little comfort in this text. The value of a creative endeavor cannot and should not be compromised. It would be a great surprise to find that Henry Moore had vulgarized his sculpture to please his representative or gallery, or that Mondrian altered his style or artistic convictions to achieve a broader market. In fact, it is our experience that there is no such thing as successfully "styling down." All other things being equal, esthetic superiority usually sells better than mediocrity.

However, no man is the first and last judge of his own design, and this year's masterwork may look very questionable when viewed from the vantage point of several years hence. The marketplace, by and large, has good taste, and each year a larger segment of the buying public is better educated to select. Marketing will demand some compromise of method, perhaps of attitude, and certainly requires that you expose yourself to the judgment of others and evaluate their comments and reactions. At no time, however, should it demand that you stop being yourself, or that you give up the effort to become more skilled, more productive and more influential.

# Characteristics of the Craft Market

While the marketing of automobiles has a great deal in common with the selling of crafts or beans, each type of marketing activity has its own peculiarities and considerations. For this reason marketers almost invariably specialize in one area of sales. It is well to know the characteristics of the market you are entering before venturing forth with your salesman's hat firmly fixed on your head.

In interviewing salesmen over the years, we have noted that there is a type who believes and repeats the old saw, "A good salesman can sell anything!" What he is saying in effect is that a skilled motivator can motivate anyone to do what he wants. Granted, but too often the man who says it means that the product is secondary. With this we do not agree. Product knowledge and specialized understanding of a given market area are essential. An understanding of some of the more universal qualifications which apply to the marketing of crafts, as well as a thorough knowledge of your own product, are basic in presenting your product to best advantage or teaching others to sell it.

Craft goods are, by definition, limited production goods. In essence this means that there are no expensive tools or capital equipment needed to produce a single item. Certainly the equipment of a pottery can easily run into thousands of dollars and can be used only to produce a given type of pottery. By extensive tooling which demands high levels of production, we mean, more exactly, a single tool that will produce only a given item.

For example, if one decides to make an injection molded plastic doll, the mold alone might cost $20,000. It can be used only to produce that doll. If the manufacturer's tool amortization on each unit is 50¢, then he must produce 40,000 dolls before the tool is paid for and must therefore use mass marketing techniques to sell them.

In the crafts such problems do not exist. The cost of specific tools, if any, can be amortized over short runs. The reason that the doll manufacturer invests in expensive molds is to keep prices down. He expects that, by making a product more cheaply through heavy tooling, he can achieve a better price ultimately, and therefore higher profits through volume. If he fails to achieve a very high level of volume, his cost per piece produced will be exorbitant and he will lose heavily.

It is conversely true as a general rule that goods made with few or simple tools will not be as efficiently produced, and that the prices will be higher per unit made, even if volume greatly exceeds expectations. The product, then, must have some qualities which will justify that higher price to the buyer. The story comes to mind of a search, some years ago, for some indigenous Mexican pottery. A friend and I had seen in museums work of centuries past which we felt to be salable, but when we inspected the pottery in the local marketplace, all that could be seen were very bad reproductions of Walt Disney figures. The Indians had decided that such figures were popular, and that if they could make them, they would enjoy a mass market.

They could not, of course, compete with the mass producers in either price or quality, and they lacked any background for realizing that the slick figures they had adopted as their models were, in concept, slick. They sold very few of their crude figures and only to people whose background was as limited as their own. Once back to their own style of craft, they were able to achieve a very select, limited market, but a far greater demand than they could possibly satisfy. Their indigenous figures were far better because they were using an indigenous technique to produce artifacts of a culture they understood. They were masters of both the conception and the craft to the extent required by their objective.

We can cite then, as the first characteristic of the craft market, that it is a "limited market." The term "limited market" should discourage no craft producer. Don't confuse "limited" with "small." As a nation, the United States alone (and your market is becoming less and less bounded by the U.S.) will shortly reach a population of two hundred million people. If a craftsman could reach only 1/100th of 1% of this national market and sell twenty dollars at wholesale each year to each person in this segment, his business would be a very substantial $400,000 per year! And we are not considering markets of 1/100th of 1%, but perhaps, even now, a potential buying public of anywhere from 10-20%. Each year this market grows. It is obvious that limited markets for the limited producer are anything but small. The problem is to reach them and exploit them efficiently. Fortunately, it is far easier and less expensive for you than for the mass producer.

We next come to the consideration of the type of goods to be created and sold to this specialized market. Generally speaking, goods which are essential to the basic needs of many people sell in direct proportion to the universality and urgency of the need. Where such needs exist widely, production means to satisfy them develop on a mass production scale. It is safe to say that craft goods rarely satisfy a functional demand today. The craftsman is dedicated to producing and selling either non-utilitarian goods or goods bought for non-utilitarian reasons. For example, nobody actually needs a flower vase to keep flowers. In many parts of the world where flowers are loved and used as a prime object of home decoration, they are shown in the home in tin cans or old bottles. It is therefore custom that makes a woman buy a five dollar glass vase in our society. Similarly perhaps, it is the esthetic need, and a need for status which is no less valid than a utilitarian need, that the craftsman satisfies in selling her a handsome piece of blown glass for $50. Similarly, whereas a cup is a necessity in the American home, a $2 cup is not! A functionally adequate cup can be purchased for fifteen or twenty-five cents. Thus, any cup over that price must justify itself on the basis of other than utilitarian qualifications.

The craftsman must concern himself with these secondary, generally esthetic qualifications, and succeed or fail on the basis of his success in appealing to these secondary motivations. He can never, however, fail to recognize and meet the functional demands which will be made upon his product if he is making a product which suggests that it is functional. A $2 cup from which the customer cannot drink comfortably will not sell, however unique it may be.

We can summarize by stating that the craftsman generally does not produce goods because they primarily fill a widespread functional need. The entire productive history of mankind is an account of how man continues to develop new and better ways to fill his material needs with less and less work. Initially, one might think that craft production was flying in the face of an historical progression, but its renaissance is perhaps due to the fact that sufficient leisure has been developed to allow for a productive process which can bring pleasure, rather than greater function, into our lives.

We noted above that mass-produced goods tend toward sameness. These are considered increasingly vulgar or common (in the true sense of these words) by an increasing part of the buying public. A man whose job is an impersonal function in a huge, impersonal corporation, and who probably lives in a mass-produced house and drives a mass-produced car has increasing difficulty in achieving any distinction. Moreover, he has fewer and fewer areas in which he can express himself through the selection of his surroundings. This is true at almost any socio-economic level. The things the family chooses to surround itself with are, however, different at each level. Having a matched set of inexpensive cups may be sufficient at a very low economic level to establish distinction. At the upper income levels Mrs. Consumer may purchase $2 or $5 teacups. There is, then, a competitive "floor." Being unable to compete in providing basic functional goods, the craftsman must create a design or style such that its distinction and the distinction it imparts to the owner are seen to be the chief reason for the acquisition of the handcrafted item.

This situation demands a great deal of the craftsman as a designer. In fact, his success in the marketplace may well rest principally on this talent.

Thus, in considering product development with a view toward selling the resulting product, the motives of status and distinction, along with a recognition of the consumer's desire to exercise his own taste, must be kept uppermost in the craftsman's mind.

Some artistically abominable pottery comes to mind which was very much in vogue a few years back. It was, however, immediately recognizable as both "new" and "expensive." It sold well. Fortunately, new products can be tasteful and still different. Thus the demand for "distinction through acquisition of the distinctive" becomes a second characteristic of this market. Simultaneously we must recognize that the "useful" item, or more exactly, the item with an excuse of function, will be the better seller. For example, a ceramic ashtray becomes an object of home decor, but further, it performs a needed function. It will be used and washed often. It will thus be broken and replaced more often than a purely decorative bowl. Ashtrays are used in multiples, whereas only one decorative bowl of a type is likely to be used in a single room. Furthermore, the ashtrays are more likely to be noticed by persons other than the purchasers and can, therefore, contribute to the purchaser's status more readily. All of these considerations are contributory to the fact that, in the craft market, ashtrays are highly salable. Without stopping to think of why, the retailer knows ashtrays sell better than bowls and he will be more likely to buy them, or to buy more of them.

One suspects that our Puritan heritage, which rejects "show" as waste, may be responsible for the wider acceptance of the item that has some functional excuse for its existence.

We are, then, beginning to define an idea of the place of the craft piece in the American market. It is not basically utilitarian in most instances. It functions, if successful, as a basic and increasingly needed device for establishing individuality and status. It would be unfair to say that it stopped there. The craftsman, because his risks are smaller than those of the manufacturer, can innovate and bring the new and better design to the fore. In fact he must, because unless his items are distinctive, they will not be accepted. With an increasing flow of foreign goods made in less developed societies coming into the States, the distinction of handcraft alone is no longer enough. Fortunately, there are many things which cannot be efficiently accomplished by machines and many techniques which remain peculiar to the individually produced item, and an educated public is becoming more aware of the difference and more responsive to good design.

If you accept the fact that the product must sell on its merits, and that those merits are generally esthetic in nature, you must also accept the fact that there is a limit to what you can do to sell your product, as opposed to what the mass producer can and must do to sell his. Perhaps the most vivid illustration of product sales in the absence of qualitative product validity is the pushing of the multitude of grotesque, high-volume plastic toys which are vomited into the marketplace each pre-Christmas season. The tooling cost involved in the making of one of these toys can run into tens of thousands of dollars, and is often as high as $100,000-plus for each. More important, they must be produced for the Christmas rush well in advance. A tremendous inventory is built up and owned by the manufacturer with a resultant high risk. A manufacturer of one such war toy, we are advised, has committed himself to nearly $200,000 in pre-Christmas television advertising for a single year to insure his sales. He assumes correctly that he cannot depend on the salespeople in the stores to sell them. He must *force* sales, through creating a demand. The craftsman does not have this type of option. The craftsman cannot engage in such mass selling techniques, even to the extent of important advertising in national magazines. He must depend largely on a human chain of communications; himself to retailer to consumer. Fortunately, the caliber of personnel available to sell his product in the stores is better, at least, than the toy merchandisers' helpers in the discount houses.

The craftsman can and must promote himself and his product, but he cannot depend on promotion alone to achieve success for him. He simply does not have the volume of gross profit to employ mass media successfully on a paid, predictable basis. Thus, many modern merchandising techniques cannot be considered in the craftsman's marketing efforts. Yet the omnipresent examples of mass sales techniques have a lot to teach him.

There are many more basic techniques for selling, however, than reliance on mass media. They are, in essence, the marketing techniques which preceded reliance on mass sales techniques to move mass products. Much of the work done by big business can be used by you in selling your goods. Here are a few of the basic techniques you can use:

1. You can sell, even nationally, if you're ready, through national salesmen.
2. You can exploit specialized supplemental markets which are too small for the large producer to tap profitably.
3. You can tell a forceful personal story which keeps your personality in your product. (Big industry can't begin to compete here.)
4. You can use a short, personal line of communication which preserves your message and your thinking.
5. You can equip your relatively few salesmen with real facts and motivate them with imagination and excitement.
6. You can publicize easily and even perhaps advertise profitably within limits.

And let the giants help you. The U.S. Department of Commerce has studied almost every kind of business from a technical and sales point of view. Literally thousands of reports in the areas of product development, marketing, and sales are available to you for almost nothing. Write to U.S. Department of Commerce Field Office at 350 Fifth Avenue, New York City, for a publication list. Start reading the ads in consumer magazines analytically, for here the sales thinking of the top merchandising minds in the country is given to you daily as a textbook beyond compare. You have only to learn to read these ads for your own ends: examine them for the motivation which the advertiser is trying to create and analyze, the nature of the response that is counted on. The "bait" used in good advertising might be serviceable in selling your line.

These, and many more specific techniques will be treated at length in the following pages. Suffice it to say at this point that if your product is basically valid, the fact that you are a small producer does not disqualify you from achieving success in the market. Others have done it and are doing it every year.

# 2.

# Manufacture and Sell a Line

Perhaps it is due to the attitudes common to the crafts and the fine arts, or possibly it is the system of the "craft show" in which individual works of the craftsman are submitted, which has led the craftsman to think in terms of the "piece," the individual masterwork. Whatever the reason, upon entering the marketplace at other than the gallery level, it is an attitude which must be disregarded. Your aim, except for a few very special outlets and "special events" showings, is to create sales directly, and thus we shall examine the reasons for producing a line in terms of sales.

First, let's define a "line." Essentially a line is a group of products having some immediately distinguishable characteristic in common. The items can be sold in the same place at the same time (or at least offered to the same buyer). Take a common example: Chevrolet cars. A dealer offers four different passenger car sizes, plus trucks. Within each size he offers many models and each model comes in a great diversity of colors, options, interiors, etcetera. Yet, he carries the Chevrolet "line." There is, however, consistency. Perhaps the most recognizable level of consistency is style. While there may be great differences of appearance between the different models, there is certainly a strong, identifiable family characteristic. Second, they all provide a single function, in this case, transportation. Third, they can all be sold and serviced in the same place by the same dealer. Fourth, they are at least projected as holding a particular quality and price position in the marketplace which is distinguished from other General Motors cars, i.e. other General Motors "lines."

Sometimes a dealer carries two General Motors "lines" and is known as a multi-line dealer.

With a line presentation, the instruction and equipping of salesmen becomes far easier. For example, in a line of pottery using one or two glazes, only one or two glazes have to be carried in sample form. One color shot will probably show both glazes attractively, allowing you to present the balance of the line in less expensive black and white pictures. If a weaver is making a wide variety of items out of one type of fabric, only that type of fabric, with color swatches, need be carried along with photos of the items. One or two pins from a related group may serve to show the technique and craftsmanship which is common to an entire line of jewelry. Similarly, the information which you must give your salespeople, and which they in turn must give their customers, is simplified. A few facts will apply to many pieces. One definition of material will suffice for all. In brief, your educational job becomes easier and simpler. A few simple and inportant facts are much more likely to get through to the purchaser than your attempt to give your marketing people a course in your craft.

Bringing this closer to home for the craftsman, we'll hypothesize a weaving establishment producing a group of fabric articles. Let's further suppose that the fabrics are particularly well adapted to pillows. Our weaver might, then, create eight different pillow designs. In a sense, if they were recognizably the work of one talent, these would constitute a line.

It would be, however, a short line. Given a first season marketing success, our weaver will wish to expand his line of pillows. Perhaps the simplest way to do this would be to use the fabrics, colors, and patterns he has already perfected for other articles. What other articles should become part of the line? The best way to answer this is to check his accounts to find out what other items are merchandised in the same department stores or specialty shops to which he is currently selling. The probability is that most departments selling pillows would also sell bedspreads and draperies. Thus, bedspreads or draperies would be a logical extension of a pillow line. The bedspreads would be taken by the same buyer buying pillows; they would be displayed so as to reinforce the effect of the pillows and might be purchased by the same consumer.

However, our weaver doesn't want to do bedspreads. Perhaps the fabric is too expensive to use in large pieces. He has an urge to create wall hangings. There are good merchandising reasons for building a single group of related products, but at the very least, when he decides to make tapestries the weaver must recognize that a new line is being added, since tapestries will probably be sold to the furniture or picture and mirror department of a department store rather than to the pillow buyer. He must realize that he is complicating his marketing. Only if his distribution is solely to specialty outlets where the same store is likely to carry both pillows and wall hangings, should he consider this an extension of his present line.

Line merchandising has some prime advantages.

How often have you walked into a store to purchase an item and noted that one group was featured over the others. That is, the store showed one line completely and presented it importantly. Most people tend to have confidence in the featured group. Let us say, for example, that you're going into a store to buy an everyday sweater. There is a small group of orlon knits, a small group of mohair and wool pullovers, and various short groups of hand knit wools, etc. Then, let us assume that one display case is full of lamb's wool sweaters in many colors, styles, and sizes. Chances are the average customer, right or wrong, will tend to compare all others with the featured line. If he lacks sufficient skill or confidence to choose between the various groups, he will undoubtedly accept the store's implied recommendation that the featured grouping is the most acceptable, as well as the best value, and buy from it. In fact, you might never have found all the small groupings of merchandise whereas you could not miss the featured line.

Thus, from a standpoint of display alone, it is well to provide the storekeeper with a broad collection and then induce him to show it importantly. In so doing, your wares will appear more important and will command greater attention. Since few buyers will order every piece you have, you must have a sufficient group to allow for buyer rejection and still have an important showing in the store. It is a natural corollary to remember that in writing an order where you expect the buyer to spend only X-dollars, you should try to sell breadth rather than depth. If he sees his display shrink, he will be more likely to reorder quickly.

A line also offers the possibility of multiple sales. Return, for a moment, to the example of the pillows and the bedspread. If the consumer sees both design-related items in one place at one time, he may decide to use the pillow and the spread in the same room and thus buy both rather than one. If the items are actually use-related, as in this case, the chances are extremely high than both items will be bought. The same would be true of a baking dish with a matching salt and pepper shaker, or an ashtray and cigarette cup. By consciously developing a related line you are not only putting yourself in a position to make more frequent sales, but larger sales as well. The retailer will be more likely to work with you because he too is vitally interested in the higher unit sales that can result from multiple sales. Your line will thus place in stores more easily than will diverse, single items.

When one is the creator of merchandise, there is a great deal of ego involved in a retail presentation of your product. This is natural but it is not necessarily bright selling. The object of placing a line in a store is to sell it, not to show how versatile you are. A single idea that is proliferated in many sizes, shapes, and items is likely to make a memorable imprint on the mind of the consumer, as well as on the buyer. This will lead to future recognition much more quickly than a tour de force of varied techniques and skills. For instance, most purchasers of ceramic ashtrays would not know a hand thrown piece if they fell over it, nor would they know stoneware. Not one in a thousand could tell a one fire glaze from a two fire glost kiln piece. However, in the better specialty shops, a high number will recognize a Heath-designed ashtray as a desirable item, and a surprisingly high number will know the creator by name.

A line builds an image in the mind of the consumer in a way that changing, few-of-a-type items never can. Actually, in practice, most exceptional items, like the Heath ashtrays, emerge from a product group and become the means of identifying the group because of commercial success. It is far easier to create recognized "masterworks" in this fashion than to guess in advance.

There is a time to go the one-of-a-kind route in the retail store, and that is the special event or "promotion" as it is more commonly called. There are few products which can be made to assume value through personality in today's merchandise world. When an alert merchant finds one, and finds that the seller will cooperate in developing a program around his product, he will generally be vitally interested. For the retailer it is not a question of how many one-of-a-kind pieces he can move but rather of how many people he can draw into his store to buy his regular merchandise. Here you can bring in "far out" work, sport a beard or work in dungarees or a gold lamé blouse, prop the display with arty photos of your shop or the kids gamboling through the pottery. The object here is to establish interest through projecting personality and it can successfully be carried to extremes with care.

Not only will the retailer want a line but your salesman—even if it's you—will want a closely related product group. Once he has sold the concept of the line to a buyer his chance of a substantial order is much greater than if he were selling disparate items. Further, he knows the facts we have outlined above and also that, given important placement for a line, reorders will be more likely to result. Reorders are profitable to a salesman. The salesman sells the product on which he can make the most in the least amount of time. Giving him a line to sell will improve his chances for profit. It will thus increase your chances of enthusiastic exposure in his hands. Furthermore, once your selling people see that you are trying to develop into a line position with your products, they will be your most consistent source of suggestions for additional items.

From your point of view as a designer and as a "manufacturer," you will soon learn that line development thinking leads to economy of creative time and production. If the majority of your production is concentrated in similar items, it will usually occasion a standardization of material, equipment, manufacturing procedures, and purchasing. Life can become not only easier but also more profitable. Fewer deviations from a standard of production mean fewer mistakes and more production per man hour of labor. From the standpoint of creativity, developing a line can prove a valuable and interesting exercise. By forcing yourself to work within the discipline of one technique, you will tend to master this technique. In developing diverse products out of the same basic thinking, you will find yourself stretching technical and design requirements to their acceptable limits. A creative worker will find great diversity within the framework of a technical or esthetic unity. There is little joy in endless variety, but great satisfaction in perfection. If there is a consistent message delivered by a good retrospective exhibition of a prolific painter's work, for example, that is it. Save the next great idea for a similarly intensive development the next time.

As your line continues to sell, keep a close watch on the items which are selling best. Most often a study of your successes will lead you to basic items in the line which can support you more rapidly than can an extensive development effort.

One item which becomes a distinctive standard by which people know your work can continue to sell for a decade or more. In many cases, as with David Gill's double handled trigger mugs, Heath's ashtrays, and Fred Braun's classic sandal, they can provide volume for years. Such repetitive volume can subsidize other development work with a minimum of personal involvement in the ongoing business on your part.

In closing this subject, one warning. A line is not a static thing. While many pieces will go on selling for years, many will not, and the producer must always work on the assumption that he has one more season of active sales. He must, then, always be testing new directions for new items or a new line with a different look or character. It may take many tries to find a successor which is compatible with the current line from the point of view of both sales and production. Furthermore, a line is never complete. If you develop a line that sells well for ten years, the buyer will ask "what's new" in the line with each new season. A "bag opener," i.e. new items, should be given to the salesmen each new season just to enable them to bring the older, basic line of proven salability to the buyer's attention once again.

While the production of a standardized line may be the first distinction between the artist and the craftsman, it will also prove to be the distinction, in many cases, between the dilettante and the serious, producing craftsman.

# 3.

## Pricing for Profit

Y ou can build a better mousetrap, get a palace to put it in on Main Street USA, and sell it to every man, woman and child in America, but if you figure your price wrong, you're going to go broke. Price is the most visible and the most widely recognized indicator of value in the eye of the consumer. In some fields where highly competitive goods vie for customers, it is considered *all*-important. In the crafts, while it is a good deal less important, it will still be one prime determinant of your ability to sell your product.

The switch from an amateur or plus-income frame of reference to a businesslike attitude is likely to be difficult. For one thing, the person carrying on a business for a second income or for "psychic" income is likely to place little or no real value on time which does not have to be paid for. In thinking "profit," every hour spent on any business-related matter must be accounted for and valued realistically.

Pressure to put out a product at a "good" price will tend to perpetuate an attitude which undervalues one's own efforts. This pressure is based on the assumption that there are more people with less money. This is certainly true when you're aiming toward a mass market, but as we have noted earlier, the crafts fall mainly into a status motivation area and are bought with disposable income. Nonetheless, if we accept the fact that the same basic thinking applies to optional purchasing, a good price, i.e. a low price, will generally result in more sales of an acceptable item and a higher price will tend to restrict its sale.

"You sell on 10%?" the incredulous immigrant peddler asks a prosperous friend. "I sell on only 1% and I'm doing fine. I buy for one dollar and sell for two." In other words, if you're doing it right, it doesn't matter whether you know what you're doing or not. The chances are, however, that if you know what you're doing, you'll be more likely to do it right. Also, there is the story about the president of a large corporation who is explaining price budgeting to his subordinates. "We keep a record of every part, every bit of material, each movement in the factory and estimate labor costs on the assembly in terms of exhaustive time and motion studies a consultant has made. Each of these is punched into our computer system, and, almost instantaneously, I can give you an accurate cost. Then my vice president and I sit down with the item, try to guess at what the client will pay for it, see if we can find out what the competition is going to bid and put a price on it that we think we can get." Pricing to what the traffic will bear is still an important element in any businessman's considerations. These two bits of folk humor point up the prime considerations in setting your prices:

COSTS:
First, you must know or project what it will cost you to make the product. Both direct (costs *in* the product such as labor and material) and indirect costs must be figured. Just as importantly, the costs you incur in selling the product must be estimated and later figured from records. Since, especially at the outset, many of these will be unpredictable and almost infinitely variable, the price you set on your own labor for example, you will need some rules of thumb. If you know what the direct costs going into the product are, labor, material, fuel, packing boxes, etc., you should at least double these costs to give you a minimum wholesale selling price.

COMPETITION:
This is the second factor. Be sure it's your competition. If there is truly nothing even remotely like your product in the marketplace, competition will be of no help but also of no importance. In most product areas something else will be competing for the consumer's money. Limiting yourself to products as nearly like your own as possible, check competition in the marketplaces where you will sell.

Let's take a look at some of the common and most important elements of cost to you as a manufacturer:

RENT:
Even if you are now working out of your home or some loaned space, you will eventually have to pay rent. A local real estate agent can tell you the going rate for the amount and type of space you need. Project a fair rental as part of your overhead and figure it in when setting prices.

LABOR:
If you're paying someone else, you know what your labor costs are. Figuring your own time is more difficult. When you are working as a creator your time may be worth $10 per hour, but as a packer you can probably replace yourself for $1.75. Pick an arbitrary wage which you think is fair, perhaps $5 per hour, and price accordingly. In a relatively short time your profit records will show you what you're actually earning. Note that *pay* is a return for time expended. *Profit* should be considered separately as a return for your investment and risk taking and for your creative and managerial abilities.

UTILITIES:

Heat, light, water, telephone, etc. are all overhead costs. In some crafts they can be major. Again, if you're working at home, using ¼ of your house for business and tied into house utilities, apply the cost of those used against your product price. Most utility companies will send an estimator around to help you determine a fair share if you need assistance. On heat, for example, you would figure ¼ of your fuel bill in the costs of doing business.

MATERIALS:

Obvious and easy. Just enter all purchases and apply them quantitatively to each product, measuring as you go. Be sure to include lost or wasted materials. If you're now buying on a retail level for first samples, I suggest you figure your very first prices on buying in larger, more economical quantities that you anticipate using once you are really shipping against orders. Chances are that if you don't reach a level quickly at which you can purchase economically, your business will be short-lived.

TRANSPORTATION:

How much will you use your car? Its cost, fuel, insurance or a portion thereof is an overhead cost which, like all other factors, can only be recovered if built into the price.

INTEREST:

Most business firms, especially while growing, find it necessary to borrow money from commercial sources. The use of money costs money. Your own money, if otherwise invested, is worth money. This is another cost that is often hidden.

PACKING:

The cost of shipping containers, packing material, and packing time can be considerable. If you are making fairly large items at relatively low unit costs, it would perhaps be best to figure this cost for each item. If not, you can include materials in overhead. A few containers purchased at retail can be shockingly expensive. Prices for packing drop quickly in "wholesale" quantity. Again, keep records on what you actually spend but project prices based on anticipated buying from a local jobber. Skimping on packing can be expensive in terms of breakage and returns. Note that an adequate inventory of packing materials can represent a substantial outlay of cash. You must then weigh the cost of money tied up against the savings you can make buying wholesale.

SAMPLES:

Samples and development are necessary but expensive. Samples given to salesmen may be broken or unsalable on their return to you. Every cost of merchandise enters into the preparation of a sample line, and more besides. Your sample costs are a part of your general overhead and should be treated as such. If special samples are prepared for a specific client or customer, his order or a separate fee arrangement should pay for them directly.

ACCOUNTING:

You will need an accountant to help you set up basic records. He should prepare a simple general ledger for you to record your receipts and disbursements. He should help you to break down your expenses by category which enables you to continually refine and review your cost/price structure. Once a quarter you will probably wish him to prepare your payroll records, taxes, etc. Similarly, each quarter, using your carefully noted business checkbook as a guide, he should prepare a statement of your business for you and review it with you. Such a constant check on your business will not only help you in pricing but will show you trends in profits and costs. Adverse trends can thus be corrected before they can do real damage, and favorable trends can be capitalized upon.

Such a review can quickly tell you how your costs are really growing and the profitability of your sales. When you start by yourself, or with a minimum staff, the *rate* of profits will probably be much higher than it will be as you expand. The cost of both additional labor and administrative time will be missing at the start. As you grow, unless you watch your profit and loss position, you can find yourself losing money.

A good accountant can save you a great deal on taxes. A first year loss, for example, can be carried forward against future profits for three years or you can combine a business loss with your family income in reporting taxes.

Your accountant can save you many times his fees from the start.

AMORTIZATION:

The tools, machinery and other property you use in the manufacture of your goods will not last forever. They represent an investment. A portion of these capital goods costs should be deducted from your profits each year as a very real cost of manufacture. Your accountant will advise you as to the most advantageous depreciation method for you and tell you how to include this cost in your overhead for pricing.

SALES COSTS:

Commissions paid to a salesman are clearly a sales cost. So is your time when selling, your travel, and the cost of photos and other sales equipment you require. While your initial costs of entertaining customers will be low, they should be in the price of your product.

ADVERTISING AND PROMOTION:

Perhaps this item is zero at first, but it will not be as you grow. A simple brochure, the first long distance call to an editor or your mailing of a publicity release saying you're "in business" will fall into this category. Going along with the rule that you promote those products which have already proven successful, it is suggested that you set aside a percentage of gross sales for this area of work. Five percent of your wholesale volume would be a fair budget.

INCIDENTALS:

Quarters become dollars very quickly. Keep a petty cash box and put in dated slips each time you draw even a few cents. Don't take cash from retail sales. Stamps and staples, postage and paper, parcel post and collect charges on shipments can quickly eat up $100.

The above will probably represent your most basic costs of doing business. Costs will vary in nature and degree with each individual entrepreneur. There are less obvious but still significant costs which should be allowed for in setting your prices.

BAD DEBTS:

Even with careful credit controls, accounts which do not pay without being forced to by collection action (which can cost you 25-50% of the amount collected), businesses which fail owing you money, etc., are a fact of business life. While the rate of these failures will vary with the general state of the economy and the type of account you sell, ¾% of your gross wholesale volume during a year may be lost on just such unpredictables.

RETURNS & DAMAGE IN SHIPMENT:

Goods you ship to your wholesale customers and even goods sold at retail will occasionally come back in unsalable condition. You may not only have to pay return freight but also to sell them as "seconds" or throw them away.

MARKDOWNS:

Every merchant makes some mistakes, and some goods will always be sold at a loss. In figuring the value of your inventory, you must periodically correct for such mark-downs by including them at their true value. Otherwise, you'll just be kidding yourself into thinking you're making more than you are.

Pricing against the competition is probably going to be your first guide, and competition will continue to be a factor in your pricing. You cannot very well sell your goods for significantly more than a competitive product and stay in business. By setting prices competitively and watching your net earnings closely, you will begin to get an idea of your own value to the business since your labor will probably constitute the majority of invested time.

If you pick a price and can't sell at that price, either one of two things is wrong: the product is unsalable or the price is too high. While the esthetic values of a particular piece are certainly going to affect its price, for the purposes of pricing against your competition (*successful* competition, that is) you should try to refrain from imputing such subjective measurements of value.

The newcomer to wholesaling is often tempted to ask a professional buyer for an opinion of his prices. In my opinion this can result in as much misinformation as valid advice. Many "professionals" will lack the judgment they need to give you a valid answer in your product area, others will habitually try to get a supplier to underprice in hopes of leaving a higher margin for the retailer, and, if you talk to six buyers, you'll probably end up with six different and confusing points of view. They will tell you quickly enough if price is your problem when you try to sell to them. If they seriously resist buying because of your prices you must then resolve the question of whether or not you can sell your product profitably at a lower price.

In this regard, it cannot be over-emphasized that you must differentiate between development cost and manufacturing cost. The cost of each first piece or group of pieces, each new experiment, will be disproportionately expensive. You must, after you produce a product you feel will be salable, try to figure out what it will cost to make it repetitively in quantities. If you are stopped by a price ceiling, you must use your ingenuity to see if you cannot figure out ways to modify your production techniques, the product, or your purchasing in order to meet the price level required to sell the product.

In production there is often a long step between the first piece or the great idea and a sensible production piece. Once the manufacturing problems are solved, you can hire other labor or use apprentices or students to perform the repetitive work and concentrate more of your own time where it can be most productive: in new creation and administration. If there is one single characteristic which separates the dilettante from the serious and successful craftsman, I would say that it is the professional craftsman's willingness and ability to take an idea from prototype to economic production and then delegate its production to others.

As you gain experience you will find your own way of judging costs and setting prices. Ed Wiener, a leading New York craft jeweler, has developed a pricing formula over twenty-two years of experience which is based on the amount of metal he uses. He will weigh his finished pieces and price them, let us say, at $11 per pennyweight of gold. This retail price includes all of the cost factors listed above plus what he considers a reasonable rate of profit. Only carefully kept records and experience have led him to this simple formula, and, because he knows how much gold he buys and uses, it is a pricing system that can be rechecked periodically against his sales to see if it is holding true or needs modification.

A normal net profit will vary considerably from one small business to another. In mass marketing operations, such as food handling, a small fraction of one percent is normal, but volumes are tremendous. As a generalization, our experience indicates that a healthy small business shipping less than $300,000 a year in the style field should net between 10% and 15% on gross volume. This assumes that you are drawing a modest salary from the business but also that you employ no other management people above the foreman level. Banks are involved in watching net returns because they loan money to small business, and your bank can probably give you valuable advice if you discuss your business profit margins and other related problems with the bank where you do your banking and borrowing.

It is important to remember that this net profit figure is the figure that is important to any business. It is the margin from which money to purchase new equipment must come; it provides money to try new experiments and to gamble on new marketing efforts. It is the money which, if part is set aside, can provide you with a cushion against losses when you make an error or when business slows down. Gross volume can be deceptively large, but unless there is something left over after everyone and everything is paid for, you're working for nothing.

Accurate pricing and an accurate assessment of your profits depend on records that you must keep. At the start simple records will suffice for your accountant to work with. All substantial expenditures should be paid for by check, and others receipted in a petty cash fund. You can similarly record monies received in the checkbook, noting the source of funds. An accurate file of paid bills, kept chronologically so that it corresponds to your checkbook, gives further information on what expenditures were specifically used for.

If you are wholesaling and billing your customers, or offering charge services to your retail customers, you will have a somewhat more complex system to cover your accounts receivable. Many basic accounting systems are possible. The one with which your accountant is most familiar will undoubtedly be the one you will use. And basic financial records will be critical no matter what sort of business your craft leads you into.

Here is a rule of thumb which you can use initially: wholesale prices should be at least double your direct manufacturing costs; and as a retailer you should double your wholesale price. Depending on what your accountant chooses to put into direct costs (generally the labor and materials that go directly into a product) and what he chooses to assign to indirect, or overhead, costs, this ratio can vary. It will serve as a basis for initial pricing, and as you develop a body of recorded experience, it can be modified.

Other generalities in pricing will apply to most craftsmen. After you have made some entries into the market and watched your sales, you will begin to price, not only on cost and competition, but on visual value. This will become a natural thing to do when you can compare a new piece or group with others you have sold well. Pricing this way can give you a plus-margin on some items and can also lead you to drop an item from sale. Due to many causes arising in manufacture, an article may appear to be overpriced. While you know that all the costs are in it, they are not apparent. If efficiencies cannot be instituted to reduce costs and price, you would do well to drop those items which appear overpriced from your line. The buyer who looks at one of these items first may take it for granted that all of your merchandise is high priced and lose his interest before he starts to buy.

After you've had your commercial baptism, you must learn to ask yourself another question each time you price new things. "Will I sell substantially more if I cut the price?" Frequently, as we all know, a low price can actually injure sales. If something is quite cheap compared with other goods which you or your competition sell, it may seem to your customer that it is of little value. If you do not feel that you will substantially increase your total profits by a reduced price, don't change it. *It is the profit on each piece multiplied by the number of pieces sold that will determine your earnings.* You may find that a 5% price cut will triple your volume on an item but leave you with exactly the same earnings. It is the total profit in which you are interested. One exception to this rule is the use of a price leader: if your shop has one item which brings people in because it is attractively priced, it may pay to make a very small profit on it in order to keep your customers buying other things which are more lucrative to sell.

So far, we have discussed only the pricing you control. In most cases you will control price: in your own retail store, to your wholesale agent or salesmen, and in the specialty markets which you will probably sell yourself. There is one situation outside of your control in which you must be aware of pricing policy, and that is in the matter of prices set by the dealers who resell your merchandise.

Since you are probably making and selling a relatively expensive and low volume product, price cutting will generally be no major problem. Yet, some awareness of its dangers is indispensable.

If your merchandise is priced to sell for $10 retail, it should sell for close to $10. A price of $9.95 or even $9.50 should not cause alarm, but if a good and recognizable item appears in a store at $7.95 you may have trouble on your hands. This is especially true if other active accounts who buy from you are present in the same trading area. If the price-cutting dealer is not near anyone else you sell and is just closing out some of your goods, let him go ahead. But if he plans to reorder your line, talk with him and try to force him to hold price on it. If he will not, even if it means the loss of an account, you're probably better off threatening him with cutting off his supply. If he continues to cut price, you're likely to lose other customers who are holding the price line and who cannot afford to seem overpriced by comparison. If you are financially strong enough to do so, it might be worthwhile to try to buy back his inventory to protect your position. Make it abundantly clear to your salesmen that you will not tolerate price cutting.

This chapter can only be closed by repeating the opening statement that, in the crafts, price *is* important, but not all-important. In figuring your new prices, err, if you must, on the high side. Nobody ever objected to a price reduction, except those few people who recently bought the items, but sometimes even a slight increase can raise quite a cry. Above all, remember that the goal is not sales but profits.

# 4.

# Sales Equipment

Imagine for a moment a pile of cut glass beads in one hand and a diamond of similiar size in the other. The diamond at this moment is a separate and precious thing. Now, think about the pile of beads with a diamond of similar size just tossed in. The diamond ceases, except on careful examination, to be something special. This example might illustrate the first thought to be kept in mind in preparing a sales kit. Try to keep your items and the ideas behind them quite separate and distinct; extraordinary quality must be seen on its own terms.

Again, let's just place that diamond on a piece of wood flooring. It is hardly a suitable background, and the stone would lose much of its apparent value; put the same stone on a piece of black velvet or illuminated glass, and it comes to life! The background shows it to full advantage. Its apparent value is increased. This, then, is a second principle: a sales presentation should be devised to accent and complement the essential character and visual characteristics of what you are offering. The spirit and function of the background should amplify the character of the merchandise you are presenting. A rawhide sandal would look as out of place on a piece of black velvet as a diamond ring might look on a piece of weathered board. The juxtaposition of seemingly inappropriate elements can be very effective but it must be conceived and executed with great imagination and skill. There must be a unifying idea. The aforementioned rawhide sandals could well be displayed on a belt of Indian silk if the idea was to sell them for evening wear in conjunction with the currently fashionable Sari. An additional recognizable Indian element might have to be added to concretize the suggested connection.

The entire effect of a well-conceived and well-executed object can be lost if it is improperly presented, and, for that reason, the conception and design of a sales presentation can be as important as the products themselves. Therefore, no matter what your product is, you will need effective sales equipment.

Your sales presentation should do many things:

1. It must tell your prospect what you are selling.
2. It must tell your prospect who you are and how you feel about what you are selling (which in turn will suggest how he should feel about it).

3. It must tell your whole story quickly—buyers are busy and consumers are constantly being bombarded by "pitches" on all sides.
4. It must immediately present vital information about your product—size, colors, availability, price, variations, etc.
5. If your kit is used by a salesman who is carrying other products, it must be so designed that it separates itself, by design and mood, from the other things in his "bag," but keep it light and compact.
6. It must organize the elements of what you are offering into a unified whole rather than presenting a group of isolated objects.
7. It should create an air of excitement and uniqueness around your product, suggesting the excitement, prestige, or other benefits the purchaser might enjoy if he, in turn, offers it to his clientele.

In brief, a really good sales presentation will not only communicate information about your product, but will communicate an entire attitude surrounding that product. It must be a "stage" for your products and the personality that created the products. Most of the comments made here apply to display in a retail store as much as to a portable sales presentation. Certainly, for the craftsman selling both wholesale and retail, his sales presentation material and his retail outlet, which will in most instances serve as his wholesale showroom, should exhibit the same image and attitude.

In a sales presentation quantity of items is not the answer. If anything, redundancy of similar items tends to cheapen them. If a woman walks into a fine dress shop to make a purchase and finds the rack with her size, she will find various dresses, one of each, hung there for her review. If, on the other hand, she enters a "discount" establishment, she is likely to find many garments of a kind, all grouped together. Where redundancy in display occurs, it is almost always suggestive of a "price approach." In a retail store situation, every item that is for sale must, in one way or another, be displayed or represented because the ultimate consumer or user will make the choice.

If the buyer is convinced by an idea, he will most frequently go on to buy an assortment. Thus, while all the items and variations must be explicable through what you present, the presentation of each item in every variation will only serve to make your selling slower and more confusing. An economical presentation which tells the whole story, or at least the important facts of your story, is the best presentation. By not heaping a confusing variety of products on your customer, you have more time and space in which to convey attitude.

For purposes of illustration let's assume that you are a glassblower, and that your current line consists of six tumblers, six stemware shapes, and six larger pieces. Let's further suppose that you make your line in three colors and offer it with an acid etched dull finish and in a bright fire-polished finish. Your sales equipment might—almost inconceivably—consist of as many as 18 pieces, each in three colors and two finishes or a total presentation of 216 pieces. This would be a confusing mess at best. At minimum, it could consist of one each of eighteen pieces (or representations) assorted to show the different qualities of each type of piece and all colors assorted in both finishes. Even eighteen physical samples would prove burdensome in a buyer's usual small space. They would require too much time to pack and unpack and would be cumbersome, so you can substitute photographs or some similar device to represent most of the shapes.

The type of product you are producing will determine the kind of sales material you will create. At one extreme, the jewelry salesman can carry a line of a hundred samples in a simple presentation case, so that each item can be examined. A man who makes architectural pottery can hardly carry, or expect his salesman to carry, even a single piece. In the case of the jeweler, it may only complicate matters to show the entire line in sample form and, certainly, such a sample kit would be expensive to duplicate for several salesmen. It might suffice if the jewelry line were exhibited by ten different categories of items, and then ten samples plus photographs. The photo of a ring on a beautifully manicured hand, taken with proper lighting, will convey an attitude of elegance which may not be communicated by the actual sample in a sample case.

In the case of architectural pottery, a few tiles showing body and finish could be nearly as effective as an entire piece, and the pieces—or many of them—could be photographed in appropriate and suggestive settings.

In the case of handwoven textiles, each quality must be shown to exhibit weight, "hand," drape, and other characteristics of the fabric, but smaller swatches could be used to show color.

On a recent European selling trip during which I visited stores in six countries and traveled by air, I had to pack samples to represent about 700 South American handcrafted items in a single thirty inch case. I decided to put in a four by six foot Peruvian wool rug of limited salability but of great interest as a selling prop. This rug covered linoleum topped desks, formica shelves, a polished teak table, and glass display cases. It was my stage. Ceramics and crude wood carvings, which would have looked bad on many slick, hard surface materials, suddenly recaptured some of their native character on the rug and were bought. Of the twenty odd buyers who were sold, only one bought the rug—the largest item in the display! It was, however, actually the most valuable item in my bag. The shiny, black Cadillac on the used car lot sells a lot of used Fords. Your presentation must suggest. It need not fully illustrate. As a society we are conditioned to accept a representation of a totality as a communication of that totality. We are educated to project the elements not clearly visible in a representation.

Educated to such abstractions, we tend to supply not only missing details, but also to project given or suggested characteristics from an abstract communication. In advertisements, the radiator of a Rolls Royce imparts an attitude of the "quality" life to a case of whiskey. A hazy city skyline behind a martini glass suggests a whole picture of sophistication, the cocktail hour activity for which the advertised gin is appropriate. We have been taught to fill in the details that we want to find there.

Photographs have become the accepted basic means of presenting merchandise in the absence of the product itself. The two examples given above refer to photographs, and in both cases the pictorial, graphic presentation is superior to the display of the actual object. If the case of whiskey were shown on a shelf, it would hardly compel buying. The martini, mixed and frosted on display, might induce consumption, but it is questionable that it would induce selective consumption. *Selective* purchase is what you are trying to promote. As you have noted above, the decision to buy depends as much or more on what the product suggests or connotes as on what it is. Photographs, unless planned to do otherwise, almost always carry a host of information in addition to the principal representation. Think about a family snapshot taken out of doors. It usually captures the ambience: a picnic, the beach, an evening at a party, or whatever. It tells relative size: people as compared to familiar objects around them and to each other. Since people change and grow, it can roughly establish time, and often time of day. If taken in color, it can be a more accurate rendering of a moment, but if not, memory and familiarity with the pictured objects will supply the color information.

It is exactly the same with the photographing of a product, except that with some forethought, the situation can be altered to make it suggest what you would have it suggest. Let's photograph a hand thrown stoneware casserole. First, we'll think about what it is used for, in this case, food, and preferably baked food. Second, it is probably meant for casual dining. Third, we want to give it a hefty, hearty look to accent its natural materials. Finally, let's decide we want to make it look elegant. All this can easily be communicated in one picture.

First, it would be photographed filled with food (at least partially), in this case perhaps a baked chicken casserole, accented with some brightly colored garnishes. If filling the casserole with food somehow obscures an important part of its appeal, put two casseroles in the picture, one with food and one without. To give it a casual air, show it on a casual surface; on rough planks, or in a setting with bright, obviously informal placemats. Elegance can be suggested easily, perhaps with a thin stem glass of white wine partially shown, or with fine sterling as a part of the setting. The inclusion of any familiar object which connotes elegance will make this suggestion. Other items can be introduced for other purposes. The cork of the wine bottle or a fork will show scale. Perhaps several mugs of the same ware can be grouped in a less important area of the picture to show other glazes in which the casserole is available.

We now have a picture of an item. We see that a simple picture can be made to communicate more than a physical description of the item itself. Perhaps you will want to make such photographs of several of your most important pieces, but it will probably be too expensive or time consuming to make pictures of all of your items in this manner.

The second kind of photograph must show logical groups of merchandise. It is purely descriptive rather than "editorial" in its intent. It is the purpose of the group photos to do at least two things: to show how the various items relate to each other, both functionally and esthetically, and to suggest display possibilities to the retail outlet. They can and should communicate as much of the attitude of the ware as the individual photo, but with many items in the picture, you will necessarily have to eliminate many props like the placemats or the wine glass. You will undoubtedly wish to include some props, if only to show size, such as a few pieces of fruit in a bowl. Backgrounds can be as suggestive as in the individual photo, but should be subordinate. Groupings should be logical. For most items this means grouping by function: all drinking mugs, tumblers and glasses together, perhaps along with pitchers; all serving bowls and platters together to show various available shapes and sizes, etc.

There are other kinds of presentation materials and photos which will help you or your salesman to sell.

Take pictures of people making things to show that hands and not machines are responsible for what you sell. Show pictures of interesting aspects of your studio or of your methods, or come in close on photos which can show the distinctive features of your product. If you have a shop of your own, show in pictures how you display your merchandise, or if not, try to get pictures of how other people have shown your goods well. Merchants, like everyone else, sometimes lack confidence and can be "sold" by seeing what others have done.

Finally, after you have all your pictures together, put proper descriptions on them. It has always been my experience that such information should appear on the back rather than on the face of the photo, since properly planned photos have already told the person viewing them most of your story. Verbal descriptions are there for confirmation, information, and price. You will notice that up to this point, we have not mentioned price. This is as it should be. In selling, the whole idea of what you have created, the actual goods and details about them, must be communicated before getting into the matter of cost. Of course your price is reasonable!

A description should specifically include, at the very least, the following information as it applies to your products. It should be listed in simple tabular form:

1. The number of the item.
2. The name of the item.
3. Size(s) shown and other sizes available. (Indicate which item is actually shown. If other items are near-identical, all sizes need not be shown.)
4. Capacity, if any, as separate from measurement.
5. Full information about materials, i.e. not just "stoneware," but "hand thrown gray stoneware with flocks of manganese, high fired to withstand oven temperatures safely."
6. Colors or finishes. These must be shown in photos or samples, but should be restated. Some people attempt to romanticize color names—seafoam green, sand tan, lobster orange, etc.—in an attempt to establish an attitude or mood. I've found it a nuisance to buyer and seller alike and favor a straightforward and explicit color description.
7. Standard packs and combinations: if you have bought a carton to hold eight mugs or a dozen pair of sandals of a type, so state. Your standard pack is then eight or twelve and that is the way your goods must be bought. If you do not sell the cream pitcher except with a sugar bowl, so indicate on the description of the set. Show them, number them, and price them as a unit. If your standard packs are reasonable for the type of customer to whom you are selling, you will seldom, if ever, lose a sale and may be able to increase an order significantly.
8. Show price. For the purposes of a wholesale presentation kit, this should be a wholesale price. Among other things, the buyer will be working with smaller figures and tend to build his order to a larger amount.

With good photos and such information on them, you have a very portable selling tool and one that can even be mailed when it is impossible to make a personal presentation.

The making of photographs is too often considered some sort of occult art. For the uninitiated the first inclination is to buy them. This is a perfectly sensible reaction, and, if you are fortunate enough to have a photographer who can work creatively and interpret what you want him to say, you're in luck. A straight commercial studio is, however, seldom an answer as they are usually concerned only with making a "clear representation" while a selling photo should be a great deal more than that. It has been my experience that, most often, craftsmen know people who can take pictures and who are, like themselves, creative people. You can often trade your ware for a friend's photo work. Remember that what you want is not alone a matter of technical competence, but pictures which will communicate your ideas. So, regardless of who will actually make the photograph, it is up to you to carefully think out what you want, to visualize it and prepare for it. Finally, be there when it is made and don't hesitate to inject yourself into the process of making the picture. Any normal person can learn the mechanics of making photos, and the best way to begin your photo education is to watch somebody else do it.

If, because of cost or the unavailability of the kind of photographer you want, you are faced with making the photos yourself, try it. The best tools for making still life photos are still not automated, but as a photo magazine editor once remarked to me, "a mechanical brain is better than none," and good photos can be made with autoset cameras. Polaroids and non-focusing types are not, however, very suitable tools for making the type of prints you will want. Polaroid photos are difficult to reproduce and non-focusing cameras do not generally allow you to work closely enough.

Ideally, a camera for making sharp still life "product shots" should have a number of features. Your camera should provide some sort of ground glass viewing to allow you to compose accurately through your lens. While a flexible view camera which allows the photographer to correct perspective and adjust the zone of sharp focus is best for still life photography, excellent results can be obtained with "rigid" cameras, given a bit of experience.

All other things being equal, the larger negative will produce the sharper print, so that a 35 millimeter camera, which is the most popular type today, is not necessarily the best answer. A camera making two and a quarter square pictures, such as a Rollei, would normally be considered minimal. Again, it is a matter of the user and the degree of care exercised. Some superb still lifes have been made with good 35 millimeter cameras that meet none of the above specifications. In the absence of automated exposure, the best answer is to spend an hour learning to use a good exposure meter. You will then be able to adjust any camera for accurate exposure with all types of film.

Photographers' studios generally present a confusing array of lights, diffusing and reflecting screens, etc., and to the professional such lighting tools are probably more important than the camera itself. Lighting sets the mood, delineates shape and defines texture. It can even control color. The professional photographer, moving from one complex problem to the next in the course of a day, must be able to control light at will. You don't need all of these skills. The best light in the world, especially for color photography, is hung in the sky from morning until evening. While it does not admit of the same degree of control that you can achieve in a studio, sunlight, either outside or in, is the simplest light for you to use. During the middle of the day it provides you with a clear hard light that will pick up texture. If the shadows it makes are too deep, try reflecting sunlight into the shadows by using a white cardboard or board covered with crinkled foil. Sunlight can be made softer by diffusing it with a screen of cheesecloth or similar material. Even jewelry and bright metal objects can be shot successfully out of doors if you can build a "tent" of white tissue and put your objects under it. The

elimination of harsh shadows and dark reflecting surfaces allows the sculptured nuances of polished metal to be seen.

Sunlight, to most amateur photographers, means direct sunlight, but for
most black and white purposes direct sun is not necessarily best. If you look
at good magazine photos, you will see that many pictures and most fashion
shots are made in partial shade or by reflected light.

The soft light of an overcast day can be excellent for product photography. When exposing color film in the shade, be careful that the surface reflecting the light or filtering it is not colored.

Light under a green tree is very likely to result in a green picture. Sun
in the morning and evening has a warm glowing quality and is highly directional. Some unusual effects can be achieved at the beginning and end of the
day. To see how your ware will look in a given light, simply force yourself to look at it. While merchandise can look excellent against selected
natural backgrounds (look at the good advertising illustrations for some
ideas), a plain "professional" background is easily achieved. No-seam paper in rolls 108 inches wide is available through display materials suppliers
in most cities. While it comes in dozens of colors, white is the most useful
for most subjects. A roll costs only about $8.00 and will last for many
"shooting" sessions.

When loading your camera for black and white pictures, choose a slow
film for good detail. Panatomic X and Plus X are both excellent choices,
and the old standby Verichrome is preferable to high speed films in most
instances. Using Kodacolor film, amateurs can achieve excellent color prints
with little difficulty. Instructions are packed in most films which give the
user the necessary basic information.

In addition to your camera, a light meter and film, your most important
accessory will be a tripod stand for your camera. A sturdy one, rather than
a slick, portable job is what you want for still life pictures. Add a cable
release and you have a set-up to make slow exposures without showing
movement.

Most of the aforementioned equipment can be obtained second hand at
very substantial savings. One of my treasured working cameras is an auto-
matic Rolleiflex built about 1937. While it lacks some of the latest con-
veniences, it cost me only about $50, whereas a new one would be over
$200. It is safe to say that the pictures it makes show no age. Second
hand precision equipment, purchased through a reputable dealer who will
give you a trial period in which to inspect and test the purchased equipment, can be a very sensible way to buy.

So much for exposing the film. Once you've taken the picture, you have
to have it processed. Kodak does an excellent job on color film and prints
(though if you are going to use color prints in quantity, you may be able
to save some money with an independent laboratory). The same, unfor-

tunately, cannot be said for the processing of black and white pictures by most commercial "drugstore" services. Where there are professional photographers, there are professional processing laboratories which do excellent work and will follow instructions in making prints for you. Depending on the laboratory and area, eight by ten prints will cost from about $1.00 to $1.50 each, but the quality of professional work needed to present your merchandise effectively is well worth this price. A few of the major New York City laboratories which are reliable and will work by mail are:

Bernard Hoffman Laboratories, 78 Madison Avenue
Leco Photo Service, Inc., 11 West 42nd Street
Modern Age Photographic Services, Inc., 6 West 48th Street
Weiman and Lester, Inc., 106 East 41st Street

A request to any of them will bring instructions for working by mail and price lists of their services. Local inquiry may well develop a contact for you with a professional laboratory capable of doing quite satisfactory work more conveniently.

Direct experience is certainly the best way to learn picture making. Your local dealer, your processing lab and advanced amateurs (who love to talk about their hobby), can all give you information and hints at the start. The reading of a basic text such as Kodak's perennially excellent *How to Make Good Pictures* can help. However, the best source of information will be the pictures you make. Once mastered, photography can be one of your most important sales tools.

The descriptive material for the photo backs can be prepared in many ways; office duplicators and photocopiers are the easiest means if available to you. Carbon copies made on a typewriter and sprayed with the fixative that graphic artists use will also work well. This material should be brief and clear, and information should always be presented in the same patterns.

While I have attempted to lay down some guidelines to help you in the preparation of proper sales equipment, no single system will be right for all cases. The most important consideration, then, should be to keep your sales equipment flexible. If you try selling with it yourself, as you must, you will find out how it can be improved.

You can see what is wrong when, during a presentation, you find that you cannot fully illustrate your point. Certain samples and photos will come to seem redundant and you will find yourself skipping them. YOU are the one who must design and test your sales equipment *before* giving it to your salesman. If you rely on salesmen or representatives to tell you what they want, they will give you as many directions and suggestions as there are imaginative men among them. You should listen to them, weigh their requests and ideas against your own experience and then act. Remember that a camel is a horse that was built by a committee. You must set the tone, mood and direction for your presentation, as you did for the merchandise which it presents.

A price list is the easiest part of your sales equipment to prepare, and one you will find most useful. A price list is basic for the merchants to whom you sell, and one should accompany every bill that you send out to serve as a reorder guide for the purchasers. Being cheap (a single typed page can be printed for $10 per thousand or less), you can give them out freely when requested. If you can illustrate a price list, perhaps with a simple line drawing to indicate shape, it will help your customer. Such an illustrated price list of the simplest kind can forestall for a while the need for a more expensive catalog. Similarly, you can set up a price list as an order form, making it necessary for your salesman to fill in quantities only and to mark a few flexible facts like size or color and thus speed up his selling. Once the first make-ready is made in printing, larger quantities tend to be very inexpensive, and the more use you can make of a simple tool like a price list, the less it will cost you for each one.

Professionals like to do business with professionals. The presentation you make, or the way in which your representative presents your products to a prospective account, can give the impression of a well thought out professional presentation, or can mark you as an amateur. By building confidence in your prospective customer through a professional presentation, you will be strengthening his confidence that your business relations will be just as well handled and satisfactory to him. Apart from the actual goods which you have to sell, nothing can build your business more quickly than an admirable presentation. It is well worth both the time and the money that you will invest in its preparation.

# 5.

# Recruiting a Wholesale Sales Force

The term "salesman" brings up a host of unpleasant connotations, most of them false and outdated. However, an image of aggressiveness remains, and should. You will have to develop the qualities of a good salesman, yourself, or you will have to learn to live and work with those who have such qualities. A salesman today is no longer a man with a big ego and checked vest. He is usually a professional whose principal skill is persuasion. The better he is, the less aggressive he will appear, but if he lacks confidence, he cannot sell. There's an old adage among road salesmen: "If you sell it to him and he doesn't resell it, you sold it to him. If you sell it to him and he resells it, he bought it." This cliche says in effect that the salesman is not going to get credit either way, so he'd better do what he, himself, thinks best. The buyer doesn't have to love you to reorder, he just has to make money on your goods.

Most merchants are not noted for being venturesome. Often they need a solid push. There is nothing wrong with you or your representative pushing your product. It only becomes an immoral act when you are pushing something that you know is worthless. At times you must assume that you know more about what the retailer can sell than he does, and if you are confident, *sell*. In making your plans, first stop and think of what he wants from a product: a traffic builder, profits, an attention-getting device which will bring people in, or prestige. The good salesman will try to guess beforehand what it is beyond the articles themselves that will make your product attractive to the customer and then build your sales story on what he thinks the buyer wants to hear. Will the local press support the customer's efforts to sell your products because you're local? Colorful? Superior? Can he have a gallery-like showing of your things that will bring people to his store? Will your line lend an air of prestige and elegance to his other good, but less interesting, products? The salesman must anticipate the customer's wishes and show him how these wishes can be served by your product.

Finding the right man to handle your work is very important, and what sort of man should he be? As one of my first employers forcibly pointed out to me, a salesman is one who sells. If he can't do that, the rest is unimportant. His primary qualification is not, however, his only qualification.

A man can sell you right into trouble if he sells the wrong way. He can destroy you in many ways if he's not the right man.

The first question you should ask yourself when first talking with a potential candidate is whether or not he is the kind of person you want to have representing you. He will be identified with your firm, in fact, to most of his customers he *is* your firm. Most of the people he calls on will know him, but few of them, at least initially, will know you. Don't automatically try to find a person like yourself. His job is not the same as yours, and his personality and presentation of himself must be right for his job. Ask yourself if the customers you do know would welcome a call from the type of candidate you're interviewing.

Second, does he call on the right kind of outlets? Normally a salesman whose services you employ will be selling various other lines of merchandise. It is unlikely that a normal commission on your line alone could support him. Will the type of merchandise he is carrying and offering also take him to the type of outlets you hope to sell? If your line is right for the quality shops in the jewelry field, and he normally carries a line which looks to you like it would be sold to discount house notions departments, even though it includes jewelry boxes, he's the wrong man. He'll spend most of his time where the merchandise he carries can be sold most easily and in the greatest quantity. If you don't fall into his prime category of sales outlet, you'll get second best, if that.

Third, does he have time to carry and sell your line? This is a difficult matter to judge for a newcomer to sales management, yet you must try to evaluate this aspect of his position. If a man with the right kind of complementary, but non-competitive, merchandise is carrying perhaps ten lines, and assuming all are equal, you will get ten percent of his time. They never are equal in practice. Some will be his strong or basic lines and you, as a newcomer, cannot expect to get as much volume from his activities at the outset as his established bread-and-butter lines. However, one way to judge is to estimate the portion of his income that you realistically expect to give him. Sales agents' earnings vary as much as the men who earn them, but a good independent agent should earn $15,000 to $35,000 per year including his expenses, seldom less unless he's relatively young in the field, and often much more.

If your man earns $20,000 per year and you think he can sell $20,000 worth of your merchandise at a ten percent commission during the first year, then you should expect about ten percent of his time to be spent on your product. At the outset, when he is investing time in placing your line, time spent can of course be disproportionately higher. In any case, a man with four or five lines plus yours is likely to be a better gamble than a man with twice that number of lines.

A realistic appraisal should be made of what he really expects your line to do for him. If he feels he can do $50,000 with your line and make $5,000 for himself, and you feel you cannot produce that much, this should be openly discussed with him. If his expectations are unrealistically high in terms of your experience and production ability, he will soon become dissatisfied and you will lose a salesman. Conversely, if the line sells more easily than he anticipates and he can place it more broadly, he will quickly find this out and his enthusiasm for selling your product will grow. You know what you want from him, but you must get a clear idea of what he really expects from an association with you. A deal with a representative is only going to work if both parties to the agreement are satisfied.

Your judgment as to whether or not a line he is already carrying conflicts with yours, again, must be a realistic judgment on your part. Let us assume that a craftsman is making batik wall hangings in a price range of $10-25. You know that the prime outlets for your wall hangings would be:

1. Better furniture stores.
2. Picture and mirror departments of quality department stores.
3. Specialty shops dealing in decorative accessories.

If one of your prospective salesman's lines is fine mirrors, there could be little question. The line would take him to furniture stores and picture and mirror outlets, though not perhaps to specialty stores. If his second line was unusual lamps, he would be selling them to furniture stores and specialty shops but not to picture and mirror departments. So far, so good. A question might be raised if he had a line of sculptured wood wall hangings, but it shouldn't be. While he will be trying to take the same buyer's money for two wall decor lines, he will also be a more important resource to that buyer who needs wall decor and will have a better chance of placing your line. Even if he had another line of fabric wall hangings which were distinctly unlike yours in design concept or even in price, this shouldn't necessarily discourage you. After all, chances are that his buyers must find accessories for Early American rooms as well as for contemporary and traditional settings. Perhaps he can buy both. Only if you feel that in most instances a buyer will make an actual choice between your product and another being offered in the same style and price range should you be concerned with a conflict in your man's bag. Then, you must judge if he will be successful enough with your line to lead him to sell it over the competing merchandise. At the very least, complementary lines such as are outlined above would indicate that he is specializing in your part of the market.

Ask for references. He should be willing to give you the names of the principals of other companies for which he sells, at least the name of the man he reports to. In some instances, he may feel that he would prefer you not to contact a particular firm, but if he will furnish few or no references, be wary. Next, ask how long he has represented these firms.

A man who changes lines often is suspect. What lines of merchandise has he sold in the past and why does he no longer sell them? Again, references might be in order to verify what he tells you, and what he tells you should be logical. The best image will be created for you by picking the right man and using him to represent you for a long period of time. Frequent changes of representation can reflect negatively on your product as well as on the man's ability, in the eyes of the buyer.

Are you considering contracting with an individual or with a group of salesmen? A group can of course mean less sales management work for you since the salesmen will probably be directed through a central office. However, it also means less opportunity for personal contact and control since the men are one step further removed. A group is more likely to have a showroom in an important market center and to visit more of the shows or regional markets that service your trade, but all this adds up to greater demands. If a man has a showroom, attends shows at his own expense, hires sub-salesmen, etc., it can mean more volume but it will certainly mean, and under the right conditions be worth, more commissions. Are you ready for a strong group effort, or will a man or two satisfy your needs for sales now? If in doubt, start small. Perhaps the only thing worse than an inadequate sales program is one which is too ambitious. If you cannot supply and service a strong sales force, you will end up disappointing both the representatives and their customers. Confidence is harder to rebuild than it is to build initially.

Finally, and perhaps the most important factor of all, do you think you can have a friendly working relationship with this man? After all, you and your salesmen are partners in a very real sense. If you can't work with him because your personalities simply don't allow mutual accommodation, you're headed for an unpleasant experience. Can your prospective representative develop a genuine respect and enthusiasm for your product? If not, he's unlikely to sell it well. Perhaps the best measure of his own equipment to sell your line is whether or not he has a vocabulary necessary to present it well. Words are a salesman's primary equipment. If he has developed a knowledgeable patter about the other lines he sells, chances are he can do the same with yours. If an educated esthetic vocabulary is really needed to sell your product, be sure that he has it. This can easily be noted as you talk with him about other products he sells or sees in the market place. He need not know all the technical and artistic intricacies of your craft as you do, in fact a concern with them will probably slow down his selling; but he should know enough to communicate your ideas effectively.

If you have some idea about the kind of man you want, how do you go about finding this paragon of virtue? Several ways are open to you. First, if you have followed the recommendations made earlier, you have, yourself, been out selling. (Your success will help you to convince a salesman to carry your line.) In your own sales activity you will have contacted a number of buyers. These buyers see many salesmen each week. Some they remember and others are quickly forgotten. The important ones, from the buyer's point of view, are the men he has done business with over a period of time and with whom he has established a good working relationship.

He should know through what firms these men can be contacted even if he doesn't have their home phones or addresses. A letter marked "personal —please forward" to a firm he represents should reach him. Ask the buyers whom they would recommend as an appropriate man to sell your line. If a buyer has nobody in mind immediately, ask him to think about it and call him back some days later. These buyers will have the knowledge and experience to make the right kind of choice of a salesman in most instances and can be of prime importance to your recruiting effort. Even if you have not actually done business with a store or buyer, a considerate approach may meet with willing assistance in your search for salesmen.

From local buyers you can perhaps find one man. Obviously, the buyer will know only the men who call on him in his territory. The selection of this first man will be of the greatest importance to you. First, if you start with only one man and he is the right person, working with him will tell you much about what you can expect from salesmen in general. And second, he can lead you to other men. Because territories do overlap and men go to the regional and national marketplaces together, men in one area will develop a knowledge of men in other areas. One firm may call in all its men to an annual sales meeting, so that the man you hire will naturally have contacts in other parts of the country. Thus your first salesman will lead you to contacts with others. If he is the right kind of man, and his judgment proves valid, he can find other "reps" in other territories for you.

The next effort might be centered around the wholesale publications that service the trade to which you are selling or want to sell. While daily or weekly publications are more often read for classified advertising than are the monthly books, your trade may have only a monthly publication. Try it. Timing is important in the placing of ads, and the best time to advertise is during a period when the selling season is over in your trade and the salesmen are likely to be off the road. A review of other similar advertising in the publication you intend to use will tell you how to phrase your classified ad. (If there is no similar advertising, it's the wrong publication.) A "help wanted" advertisement should give the prospective applicant some information about your company and the situation you are offering. It should state the kind of line you have to sell, the quality or price level of the line, the type of outlets you wish to cover and the territory available. The manner in which you intend to pay a salesman should be stated, and, to save time in subsequent correspondence with applicants, your ad must call for a full reply in the applicant's first letter. A typical advertisement might read as follows: "New England representative calling on quality gift, home-furnishings and department stores wanted to sell distinctive line of enamel ashtrays and decorative accessories. Liberal commission. Reply in full detail. Box 123." Beware of the salesman who does not reply clearly and forcefully. If he cannot sell himself it is doubtful that he will sell your product. His ability to express himself clearly, present himself in a desirable light and demand immediate action on your part are as important in assessing his suitability as the actual information his reply contains. His reply should convey a feeling of energy, genuine interest, and urgency.

In every trade there are market centers where an important segment of the trade is represented. These are generally located in the major territorial centers which buyers visit, such as New York, Chicago, Los Angeles, Dallas, Atlanta, etc. Craft marketing centers, or the closest thing to them, might be found in specific buildings in each of these centers, for instance the 225 Fifth Avenue building or the Decorative Arts Center in New York, the Merchandise Mart in Chicago, the Brack Shops in Los Angeles, etc. They are well known to the trade in the area and casual inquiry will enable you to locate them. They house not only important showrooms of producing firms, but very often the offices of top regional and national distributors.

A review of these centers will often enable you to locate a suitable sales representative on both the regional and national levels. However, unless you make a specific request, you are unlikely to find yourself a single salesman. Firms that show in such centers are generally composed of sales groups working for a single management which distributes more broadly than a single salesman. It is possible that you will find the perfect salesman on your first effort, although the job of recruiting the right salesman is likely to be more difficult than that. In any case, before you make up your mind, you can gain some experience in interviewing by talking to several.

Salesmen are, generally speaking, money motivated. Before you make an agreement with a man you must already have decided how you are going to pay him. There are various arrangements:

STRAIGHT COMMISSION:
This is the most common and generally the most satisfactory method. As you speak to merchants in your trade you will discover that the commission rate is standard or else varies within a standard range. You should work within that range. Premium commission demands generally indicate a lack of confidence on the part of the man applying for the line. For example, in the gift and decorative accessory trade a limited volume line in the hands of a regional salesman should pay a commission, currently, of perhaps 15%. If a sales representative group maintains showrooms and visits national trade

shows, it can demand and get 20% or even 22½%. If such a firm will also accept responsibility for collection, billing accounts, etc., they can ask and get 25%.

In the ready-to-wear trade, even specialty items are likely to pay only half this much in commissions. Commissions are generally payable on shipments, not orders.

### ADVANCE AGAINST COMMISSIONS:

This is sometimes called "draw." Under this arrangement a man may want a regular weekly or monthly payment of a given amount, let us say $200 per month. In your initial sales arrangements this type of agreement should be avoided. What it means is that you should be certain that a man making ten percent must sell regularly in excess of $2,000 monthly to justify your paying a $200 "draw." Certainly, you can honestly hold out to a sales candidate the possibility of a drawing account or advance arrangement *after* he has proven his ability to deliver sales. For instance, if during the first six months of employment, allowing for seasonal fluctuations, a man earns $6,000 in commissions, good business sense would indicate that you might, without significant risk, advance him a draw at the rate of $500 per month. Monies he is advanced are, of course, deducted from his next commission accounting. After a man has proven himself, a draw arrangement can be desirable from your point of view if you can afford it, since it will tend to bind a salesman to you by regular income expectation.

### SALARY:

While customary in large corporations, a straight salary arrangement for a road salesman would be unusual in most trades, especially where a salesman carries more than one line.

### OVER-RIDES:

It is conceivable that a man selling for you will provide you with other services for which he cannot be paid on commissionable earnings. For example, if your local salesman is first-rate, you may want him to act as a sort of sales manager.

He may, in such an instance, want a commission on the sales of other men, since he will be partly responsible for their effective use. This kind of arrangment is not uncommon and normally pays from 5-10% of his normal commission (i.e. if normal commission to a salesman is 10%, an over-ride on another man's sales might be ½% to ¼% on volume).

After you have a man on the job for you, how can you tell if he's doing as well as he should? Pressure to sell, if not realistic, can alienate a salesman quickly. In time experience will give you the answers. After you have had experience with a number of men in a number of territories, you will quickly know whether a man is doing his job or not.

At the outset perhaps the best gauge is your own effort. If you go out to sell for a week and you can see four accounts a day and average one out of four sold, then you're opening an account a day. However, you're not only more knowledgeable about your product at the start than your first salesman, but you are concentrating on your line alone. Allowing for his knowledge of the marketplace, then, it might be reasonable to expect him to average selling two accounts a week to start. If your rate of placement is 20 accounts a week, perhaps you should expect him to sell four to six stores weekly on your line. This evaluation of his activity is based upon the assumption that he has other lines to sell. The size of his order should, however, equal or exceed your own efforts. Unless you have a great deal of experience, he should be more competent than you are to build an order up, especially on the initial sale.

When you have two, three, or more men to compare, you will begin to develop a basis for statistical judgment. Many factors, in addition to a man's ability, enter into his ability to produce sales. One of the most acceptable grounds for judging how much of your merchandise a given territory will absorb is the territory's record as a buyer of goods of quality in relation to the national market. A compilation of the relative importance of various trading areas, states, and cities can be a valuable tool. One of the most reliable of such publications for style merchandise, and one of the easiest to use, is the *Style and Quality Market of the United States,* published by Hearst Magazines, 57th Street and 8th Avenue, New York 19, N.Y.

In setting up a marketing plan you must first know how much an area or a city *can* buy. However good your products or your outlets, there is a theoretical limit to what one area will absorb in comparison to others. An excellent guide to the relative buying power of towns and trading areas is published in the aforementioned publication. It is specifically aimed toward defining markets for products which "use better materials, superior workmanship, and at times, an improved design which price them above other products filling the same needs."

You should avoid confronting one salesman directly with another's performance, for this is just as bad psychological practice as the comparison of two children. However, such a reference can give you a partial basis for your own subjective decisions and judgments.

In judging a man's activity, remember that the number and quality of placements is more important initially than the sheer size of the order. A man who is placing your merchandise in good accounts, and who is placing the line broadly and regularly, is worth a lot more to your future growth in the territory than a hot-shot salesman who occasionally brings in the big order for a few items. If you are just starting or trying to build, the objective is growth. Immediate volume may be important, but it is secondary to establishing a sound and broad customer base of accounts that will reorder.

Once you have a sales staff, the problem is to broaden and improve it, preferably through training and experience rather than change. Keeping a salesman working and happy is also a part of your job and a few pointers may help. First, you must earn his confidence by shipping promptly and, above all, by being honest with the man regarding deliveries and the expectation of deliveries. He earns money on what you ship, not what he sells. Personal contact and rapport with a man can also motivate him to do a better job for you. If he believes you are going to grow with and for him, he'll make a greater investment of time in your line. When he does a good job, telling him so can be just as important as calling his attention to the instances in which he falls down. Salesmen, like the rest of us, thrive on earned praise. Conversely, carrying a big stick and threatening salesmen is seldom a good idea unless you are certain that you're important enough to him to make him listen (what share of his earnings do you pay him?), or unless you're prepared to lose his services. The "carrot" is generally better than the "stick," since the type of independent salesman you are likely to be using is probably a "loner" by nature, and is also likely to balk under continued pressure.

Finally, he should be paid promptly. Earned commissions for a given month should be paid by the 15th of the following month or earlier.

In summary, you will learn more about being a sales manager by trying to be a salesman yourself than in any other fashion. Put yourself literally in the salesman's place for awhile, and you will have less of a problem in thinking from his point of view thereafter.

As you hire men, agreements with your representatives should be put in writing. Like all agreements, they must be written to cover special circumstances, but the one shown below is included to serve as a general guide:

Mr. B. A. Salesman,
Marketown, U.S.A.
Dear Mr. Salesman,

I am writing this letter to confirm our various conversations and to outline the agreement which we have reached.
We are hereby authorizing you as the exclusive sales representative of the Pretty Pots line of merchandise for the states of Maryland, the District of Columbia, and Pennsylvania including and east of Harrisburg. Your representation will commence and be commissionable from January 1, 1984.
You will use your best efforts to sell our merchandise to department stores, furniture stores, gift and specialty shops, and similar retail trade purchasing for resale.
While our agreement will not preclude your selling to other types of buyers, we reserve the right to refuse such others and to sell other types of purchasers in your territory without payment of

commissions to you. We will pay you a commission of 15% on the wholesale value of all merchandise which you sell and which we subsequently ship. We reserve the right to refuse to ship a customer for reasons of poor credit, the character of the outlet, or other valid reasons. In the case of such a refusal on our part, we shall advise you in detail.

Your commissions will be due and payable on or about the 15th of the month following the month in which shipments are made. Returns of merchandise from your customers, bad debts, accounts turned over for collection, and reimbursements to customers for damaged shipments, etc., will be deducted from commissions payable to you in the month in which they occur. Such deductions will be made from your commissions on the same basis on which commissions were previously paid. A commission statement showing the name of the customer, order number, and date of shipment for each item shipped during the commissionable period will accompany your check.

If a sale is made by us in our showroom, or at the trade shows which we attend, to a customer in your territory, or if a sale is made by another sales representative to a customer in your territory, you will receive half of the normal commission.

The other half will accrue to the man making the sale. Conversely, when you make a sale in another representative's territory, you will receive one half of the normal commission. All orders taken by another salesman for shipment into your territory will be subject to your approval.

You will be furnished with samples and presentation material without charge. Please note that the sales presentation kit is valued at $50, our cost, plus the cost of the samples. You will be responsible for returning these to us in good condition less normal wear and tear at the termination of this agreement or at such time as we may request the return of your sales equipment. This agreement will remain in effect, except as modified in writing, until terminated by you or us. Such notice of termination by either party must be given in writing at least 30 days prior to the termination date.

Please sign and return one copy of this letter to indicate that this agreement as outlined herein is correct and acceptable to you. We are delighted to have you join the Pretty Pots sales organization, and I personally hope that this agreement will lead to a long and mutually profitable association.

Very truly yours,
I. M. Craftsman

# 6.

# Sales Plan and Policy

There are relatively few world-beaten paths to the doors of those who have built better mousetraps. If you have created a revolutionary, desirable, and exciting new product, it means very little unless potential purchasers know about it. While there are a multitude of ways to sell anything, the most likely way for the craftsman is through retail stores, whether his own or someone else's. Most people do most of their buying of style goods in retail outlets, and they develop habits or habitual expectations which lead them to seek out certain types of merchandise in specific outlets. These outlets are reached through the intermediary work of the wholesale salesman or sales agency group. The craftsman may be that salesman, or he may hire sales talent. In either case, it is a problem of the salesman to select the right retail outlets.

Anyone who has ever walked up Madison Avenue in New York, or through a similar "style area" of another large metropolitan center, has asked himself, how can they all stay in business? One fine men's haberdasher follows another, one women's shop specializes in tweed and leather, while another is formal and dowagerish. One shop sells nothing but butterflies, and another only raincoats. Such specialized marketing areas are few and extreme, but they do point up the problem. To the cognoscenti of New York, each shop has its own character and its own forte. What sells well in one shop might well be a failure in another.

You wouldn't expect to see an antique Spode teapot in Bonniers, a fine contemporary shop, even though Bonniers does sell teapots of quality. The problem of "outlet character" is the same, if less pronounced, in smaller marketing centers.

The same judgment that you apply to making your product must be fully exercised in the selection of the retailers who will sell it. Perhaps the craftsman is more frequently disappointed by failures due to poor outlet selections at the start than for any other reason. Many a pottery salesman has called on an outlet chiefly selling cheap, promotional types of dinnerware and accessories to find in it some superb objects made by a more or less local producer. When the buyer is questioned, he'll probably say he's just trying to help somebody out. Actually, he's helping him to fail. When you hit the right outlet, if your merchandise is valid, the buyer will undoubtedly recognize that it is his sort of product and buy it enthusiastically.

Stores are also jealous about the merchandise they carry. Let us suppose that a given brand of man's shirt is sold in New York by B. Altman and Company under their own label. Saks Fifth Avenue carries it under another label. Both stores know, I'm sure, that the other buys it, and they probably know of other outlets carrying that particular brand. Neither of these high quality stores objects sufficiently to the other carrying the line to force the salesman to stop selling the other. After all, the stores depend on him. There are few shirts of this quality offered. However, if a promotional store were selling the same shirt and it was identified with an outlet where one looks for cheaper, more promotional goods, both high quality stores would drop it.

Saks is unlikely to take a line if they know a poor outlet has had it and promoted it. Thus, if you settle for the wrong store first, you are likely to find it extremely difficult, if not impossible, to put your wares into the better store later. Early mistakes of this kind can be costly. It is often better to wait a reasonable length of time to try to place your things properly, than to take second best. If you cannot open the top account, a suitable secondary outlet may be better than none.

If you're doing what you ought to be doing, your product is unique, or at least you believe it to be unique. Next time you drive through a blue collar suburb, look at the furniture stores. They are probably loaded with junk that you wouldn't give houseroom to at any price. The fact that you can buy three rooms, complete (count them, 58 pieces), for only $299.99 isn't enough to induce you to buy. True, they carry price merchandise, but wouldn't you seek out interesting old furniture for the same price and refinish it if $299.99 was all you could spend? You would, and your reasons have various names: taste, pride of ownership, sensitivity, a quality sense, discretion. It takes a high degree of sophistication to recognize the fact that a product is unique, and perhaps better. One has to *care* about its quality to buy it if it costs more, and before your customer can care about quality, he must be taught to recognize it. Here, the retailer can perform a priceless service for you.

The right outlet will dramatize your product through display. It can lend its own particular aura of distinction to what you have made. The right shop will have a reputation for your kind of merchandise, as it services the type of customer who wants to buy your kind of product. Ask yourself, when you begin to review outlets, if they look like your product. If not, be cautious.

What kind of person is likely to buy your product? First, forget the rave reactions of all the people who have come to your studio and said "lovely, superb, I'd love to have one," etc. Forget, also, about the kind of person you would *like* to see buy it. What you have to know is the kind of person who *will* buy it. Compliments are cheap. When a customer parts with cash to take an article home, you know he likes it. If you find the same kind of person buying again and again, you have a basis for talking to the kind of shop that serves that kind of person. If you think of your product as young and highly sophisticated, but find that it sells to dowagers with what you consider to be poor taste, you had better try to tap the dowager market first. If you don't like your "image," you can locate an outlet which you do like and try to create for it.

Even in craft marketing, sex rears its head and should be briefly considered. The craft marketplace is divided into two parts, and the female part overwhelms the male buying sector. Women do most of the purchasing of consumer goods in our society, and the proportion is larger when the product is for the home or is an accessory item of dress. However, in the craft and folk art field, men do make an exceptionally strong showing. Many accounts report that men are among their best customers, seemingly having more confidence in their own taste than women, and being somewhat more sensitive to the value of handcrafted work.

Consequently don't make the mistake of thinking only of the female market. In fact, the "wrong market" from a normal male-female point of view has often been successfully exploited in the craft field. A now classic example illustrates this point. Men's neckties for sale in gift shops frequented almost entirely by women would seem to be an illustration of the right item in the wrong place. However, it turns out to be an example of marketing imagination and daring. Some years ago Julie Taylor (Taylor Ties), and soon afterwards others, began making men's neckwear of unorthodox fabrics. Wild colors, rough handwoven textures and unfamiliar shapes were the qualities which characterized these ties. Women, who are attuned to the marks of fashion, recognized them as unique and good looking. At $2.50 or $3.00, she could afford to bring her man a present on impulse, without thinking too much about it, and the conservative menswear buyers feared the item. While men had neither time, interest, nor opportunity to see them, the women were delighted to see their men wearing what they had bought. "Studio Ties" became a big business. Today, menswear shops do sell such ties to men to a limited extent. Generally if the unit price of an item is over $25.00 retail, there's a good chance a man will be involved in the final selection.

The good salesman is also a good psychologist and an imaginative researcher. In the above example he had to know or be told that there was a tie potential in gift shops. Somebody had imagination. Going beyond the obvious becomes especially important when the obvious outlets are either wrong for your product or not buying.

Before moving on to the factors which are introduced once you are selling successfully, there are a few more brief considerations which the seller must be aware of. The first is time. If an item is an impulse item, like the neckties, which will be bought quickly and without consideration, it should be in a location which gets traffic. People must see it, for they are not likely to come in looking for it. If you make an item of major cost, the location is perhaps less important, but the selling job which the retailer must do is much more demanding. Can the store and its people bring the customer to a decision in favor of your type of merchandise?

Second, try to determine the mental set of the person coming to that particular store. Let's suppose a fine women's ready-to-wear establishment catering to a high-style clientele wishes to purchase a jewelry group from you. It sounds right. When the woman is in the store she's thinking about her personal appearance and jewelry is a part of that. If, on the other hand, your product is a cocktail table, and is displayed in the same store, she is less likely to buy. At that moment she is probably not thinking about her living room, but rather about next Saturday's party. It can do little harm to sell the table to the store in most instances, but you can expect little business from your display. The shopper in a given outlet should be thinking about the general product area into which your product falls, especially if it is a product priced above the "impulse" range.

The possibility that selling the cocktail table to a women's shop might be injurious to your best interests brings up the next facet of your sales plan and policies: exclusivity. Let's assume things have gone very well and that you have found a store which shares your enthusiasm and which bought your things in the way you think they should be bought. You walk out, order in hand, with your eyes on new horizons. "If *he* bought it, so will others." But now you must think of your obligations. If the product you're making is recognizably different, and your buyer took it for that reason, you now have to protect him. He's on your team! You certainly should not sell to a similar, nearby outlet which reaches his customers.

While at the time of the initial sale you cannot be too demanding of the buyer, you can trade exclusivity for certain benefits. Later, when he reorders the line, you can become more firm in your requests. Without your ever saying it—though you shouldn't hesitate to say it if you must—he knows that there's a competitor who would also like to add successful merchandise. The things you can trade for can far outweigh the value of another outlet at times: a feature window display, a broad display of your line, a publicity effort on the store's part, and even some advertising, in rare instances. Remember that you must prove profitable to the store first, though you might try to negotiate a few concessions with the initial sale. If the store is right for you, and is interested in your goods and willing to cooperate with you in maximizing sales, go away happy and save the other store for some future possibility.

The degree to which you must be exclusive depends on many considerations. In a larger city no one merchant can or should expect to tie up your line (though some will try). Department store buyers will generally accept your selling a good specialty shop in the same trading area and vice-versa. Suburban shops often constitute another market even though they may draw generally on the same buying group. There is no harm in discussing another potential or existing sale with the buyer, but always do so positively, as though it was an accomplished fact. Ideally, he will always wish to stand alone with a unique, fine product. If his objections are strong enough to keep him from buying, let him tell you and leave yourself another avenue of escape. As long as you stand alone in the marketplace with a unique product, you should work to build a few good outlets rather than "loading" a market area.

If a salesman suddenly starts to sell more outlets in a town than you feel is logical, raise this point and question him. A man who is concerned only with immediate earnings may open too many accounts within a given area. While this will produce immediate commissions for him and quick sales for you, the competition which such action will create may well discourage your best accounts. "Milking a territory," as such behavior is called in the trade, generally indicates a salesman's lack of concern with the long range development of your sales and may be a warning that he plans to drop the line shortly. Such action can ruin a market for you for several years, and you must be alert to guard against such sales behavior on the part of any of your representatives.

The marketing process is a dynamic one. One can give suggestions, perhaps even encouragement, but there are few firm rules. Having read this far, you perhaps feel that sufficient guideposts have been set up and that the road is clear. However, if the road to successful marketing has a definable beginning, it has no end. You have, perhaps, opened a few accounts, but a few accounts for the serious craftsman do not equal distribution. Only that line which is powerfully placed through a broad market can instruct, lead, and encourage others and, ultimately, make its mark on the taste of the market.

When you seek to enter a new and broader field, you encounter new and more complex problems. As you do your initial selling, or consult with those who are doing it for you, you will begin to see that your choice of areas in which to expand can be of primary importance. You or your salesman will meet logistical problems. In functioning as both producer and seller, you have already become a man who must be in at least two places almost at the same time. You must now divide yourself between three, four, or five. In most fields the salesman must see his accounts at least three or four times per year. This means that new territories which you or your present sales staff cover must be geographically compact.

Excellent marketing efforts have been made by men who "high spotted" across the country as a way of beginning. They hit only top stores in principal cities. This can work, and work powerfully, but it generally requires money for travel and money to live on while you start putting an organization together to handle a broad promotion. Above all, it requires time. Also, if you are wrong, you have killed off your chief potential outlets across the country with your first effort.

There is also the question of shipping, especially if your product is bulky. If you have economical, direct trucking to one area of considerable potential, you might do best to exploit this area and learn from it. If mistakes are to be made, there is still a large market open to you elsewhere, and success in another market can eventually revitalize your first market.

One other common facet of the buyer's personality should be considered by you when you make your plans and set your policy. Most buyers are designers, or think they are. They will be very quick to tell you what is wrong with your products, what you need and how you should change your techniques and line. This will be especially true if you're small. You then have two choices: you can do everything that you're told (which is quite a bit since every buyer will have different ideas) and in doing so, lose your identity and probably your business; or you can tell him how bright he is, how valuable his ideas and interest have been, and then do as you please. This is not to say buyers cannot be helpful and instructive. They have a day-to-day view of consumer preferences which you do not. You've got to sift and sort what they tell you, looking for directions, leads, and ideas. Their "wisdom," however, cannot be a substitute for your own convictions, creativity, and steadfastness to a consistent image of what you want to create. You must believe in what you see with your mind's eye and create with your hand. Only when you have been convinced that it is wrong, after it has really failed, should you abandon it and begin to search again. In any case, be wary of making "specials" each time a buyer asks. There is probably no more tempting road to bankruptcy.

Next we come to sales policies, and like all rules, these must be flexible. Regardless of what he may want, the buyer will respect the professionalism of the vendor who sets a policy and sticks to it—if that policy is reasonable and workable.

At least initially your policies should follow the general sales policy which exists in your trade.

Your prices will be quoted and published as a "list" of suggested retail prices. The first thing to remember is that, at any given moment, the price list is inflexible. A fixed price schedule is certainly the businesslike way of selling goods, and the law (Robinson-Patman Act) requires that you make the same offer to all purchasers meeting the same conditions at any given time. If you try to be flexible on price, you will find that purchasers will always be trying to bargain for price, and when such a situation develops there is no bottom. This is not to say you cannot change price. Prices can be reduced when efficiency of purchasing or production indicates a possible reduction, and when you feel that a lower price will result in greater volume and overall profits. However, you then publish a revised price list which applies to all sales. Similarly if you raise prices, customers ordering at the old, lower prices should be advised of the new prices before their goods are shipped.

There is a more or less standard trade discount on all items. A store, others in the trade, or your salesman can tell you what your standard discount should be; on furniture it may be 40%-50% depending on the type of item or line. Pottery generally carries a 50% discount, candles 50% with all or part of the freight paid, and jewelry a still higher discount percentage. In addition to listing the numbers, descriptions, colors, sizes, etc., of your items on a price sheet, the terms and conditions under which you sell should be clearly indicated either on the price list itself or on an additional sheet. Such information is generally called *Terms and Conditions of Sale* and, depending on your trade, will include most of the following items: *terms* generally refers to the cash discount, if any, your customer is allowed for prompt payment or "discounting" of bills. For most giftware areas it is normally 2/10, net 30. This means that you will give a discount of 2% if the bill is paid within ten days of the invoice date and that it must be paid in 30 days. In other trades terms will vary, but any retail merchant dealing in a particular trade will advise you as to standard trade terms. If a cash discount for prompt payment is customary in your trade, give it *only* if the bill is actually paid within the discount period. Many merchants will try to take their discount even if they pay later. Bill them for the additional amounts due. While a few will resent it, you'll be respected by most of your customers for being a professional. They will soon learn that you mean what you say and more will try to discount their bills by paying promptly, giving you the use of more of your money. Remember that your money costs money to use.

As stated, these policies can be somewhat flexible, but they must be consistently so.

*The FOB (Free on Board) point* from which merchandise is shipped determines from what point the customer pays freight, postage, etc. Again, most shipments are made FOB factory, that is, they are packed and at the factory ready for pick-up or mailing. Because freight can be a substantial item of cost, some firms will make freight allowances. This is common in the candle business, for example, and frequent in dinnerware. You may wish to pay a percentage of freight, or all freight on orders that exceed a certain dollar amount as an incentive for the customers to order more merchandise each time. For example, you might allow a 10% freight allowance on all orders over $150. This offer should be a part of your price list. The same reasoning applies to the following example. You may have been selling in a home market which we will presume to be in the East. Your production has reached a point where you feel that you want to recruit salesmen on the West Coast and sell there, freight costs being about $12 per hundred pounds on your merchandise. To encourage your western salesmen, and to enable them to compete with local producers on the Coast, you may have to give your customers a freight allowance in certain areas. This must be given to all customers who meet your minimum order conditions and can be used by your salesmen to encourage West Coast customers to purchase from an Eastern source from which they may derive some exclusivity.

The promiscuous granting of credit to customers can be an expensive vice. Most manufacturers, before shipping a new account, will request credit information from the customer.

Common practice is to require the names and addresses of three firms in your trade with whom the account does business, as well as the name of his bank. Many businesses have given information to credit reporting services such as Dun & Bradstreet, or Lyons, and they will so state. If you do not have access to such credit checking directories, however, you can still politely request the aforementioned credit references. For a small producer, subscribing to a national credit service can prove expensive. Minimum rates can run $50 a month or more. Naturally, if the customer is a firm of national repute or a department store that has been in business for many years, a credit check can be safely skipped, but if not, make the small extra effort to protect your money.

A simple printed postal card, or a card typed by you, will do the credit checking job. A form letter with a stamped, self-addressed envelope is even better. A credit inquiry might read as follows:

The following organization has requested that we open an account for them and has given the name of your firm as a credit reference:
                    (name of account)
                    (address)
                    (city and state)
Any information you might furnish us with regard to the credit worthiness of this customer would be sincerely appreciated.

Patience in gaining credit information on new customers is necessary if you are to avoid expensive collection action at a later date. With proper simple credit checking your credit losses should be less than ¾% on shipped volume, and perhaps far less. If an exceptionally large order comes in from an account which you do not know, it is perhaps wise to have your bank draw a credit report on the customer. This will give a more detailed financial history of the account and will offer you greater insurance of being paid if the report is satisfactory. On this and other credit matters, even to the question of interpreting the credit information you receive, your banker can be of great help.

Obviously, if an account is new and has no credit credentials you will wish to be paid before shipping. Similarly, an account with questionable credit should be sold on a similar *pro forma* basis. *Pro forma* means that when an order is ready to ship, you notify the account and they are to pay you. You then ship. If their order requires that you actually make up merchandise for them, it would be well to ask for cash in advance before you actually produce the goods. It is difficult to turn down an order because of questionable credit, but it's better to lose the order than to lose the value of the merchandise shipped. It can be done politely, and as a customer knows his own credit position he will be sensitive to suggestions that you "have been unable to obtain satisfactory credit information on his account," or that "on advice of your bank you are holding his shipment pending payment", etc. You cannot, of course, just tell him he looks like a deadbeat.

You should establish a minimum order which is profitable for you. It costs money to pack, ship and bill any order. Not all small orders are profitable in terms of the time they take to process. For this reason, most firms—including small ones—will set a sensible minimum order. This will vary from firm to firm, but in giftware, for example, it should be from $35.00-$100.00 for an opening order and $35.00 for reorders. If a firm wishes to sample less than the minimum order, it is general practice in most craft trades to make a service charge which reflects the cost of handling a small order. This cost varies from firm to firm but is generally in the range of $1.50 to $5.00 per order. This extra service charge applies even to customers who order regularly if, on a given order, they ask for less than the minimum. In practice this additional charge will tend to force the customer to "buy up" to the minimum. Since your customers are usually business people themselves, they will understand the reason for such a charge.

All of the above policies are generally grouped under the heading of "Terms and Conditions of Sale." While no two firms will publish exactly the same terms and conditions "sheet" with their price list, one is reproduced below to give you an indication of how you might develop your own.

*Terms and Conditions of Sale*
*discount:*   all prices shown are list. Stocking dealers deduct 50%.
*terms:*   2% 10 days, net 30 days.
*packing charges:*   $1.50 on orders of less than $70.00 list.

*credit:*  customers ordering for the first time should furnish the name of their bank and three trade references.

*freight allowances:*  an allowance of $2.00 per hundred pounds is allowed on orders of $150.00 net or more and may be deducted from the invoice if paid within 30 days. If deduction is made, a copy of the freight bill must accompany payment. Orders under $150.00 net are shipped FOB factory, Yourtown, Mass.

All orders are carefully packed and signed for in good condition by the carrier. Claims for damages sustained in transit should be made upon the carrier within five days of receipt of goods. We will not accept goods returned prior to written consent by our office.

All goods will be shipped by the most suitable method unless specific shipping instructions are given. Parcel post shipments will be prepaid and the cost of postage will be invoiced to the customer.

Although we always attempt to ship an order complete in one shipment, it is understood that the balance, if unshipped, will remain on order and will be subject to the same terms as the original order.

One policy which has been peculiar to the craft field is consignment. In most areas of sale it is unheard of. Unfortunately, certain nationally known craft groups have condoned it, and some craftsmen have accepted it as a way of life. Nothing could be more detrimental as a sales policy for the craftsman. Consignment is the placing of goods in an outlet with the understanding that they will be paid for only after they are sold.

There are a hundred good reasons why you, as a vendor, should not do this in most circumstances. I shall quote only a few in the hopes that they will be sufficiently convincing to stop you from doing it.

First, your retailer's costs and risks are allowed for in the full markup he receives, so that your wholesale price already compensates him for the possibility that he might be forced to sell off your items at cost or at a loss. Second, his profit margin pays him for the use of the money he has tied up in goods in inventory; you should not be expected to finance his operation. Third, the merchant will use his best efforts to sell goods in which he has an investment. It is inevitable that he will be less concerned about selling goods he doesn't own. The consignment merchandise may be treated as a sort of orphan. He will often exercise less care in preventing damage or wear to goods he doesn't own and, practically speaking, you have no recourse if he returns your goods in unsalable condition. Finally, there's something to be said for a man selling goods in which he has confidence, goods on which he has "sold himself." If he has not had enough confidence to buy your goods in the first place, what leads you to believe he'll have enough confidence to convince his customers to buy them? If your goods cannot be sold on standard trade terms which you have set, there is something wrong. Either the goods are unsalable, in which case consignment will not help, or you are not selling them properly. You will have to find an answer to their own shortcomings, or yours, but consignment is seldom that answer.

There should be almost no exceptions to the "no consignment" dictum. However, certain situations may call for adjustments. You may sell goods to an outlet which, six months later, may be "stuck" with a few numbers, while selling others actively. If the man is a good customer and asks for an exchange of goods, you may wish to cooperate with him and either close out or reship the goods he has given back to you. However, this should only be done if he is ordering far out of proportion to his returns, and he should understand that you are making an exception. Occasionally you will find situations in which you are placing goods to serve your interests more than those of the buyer. For example, a store may be carrying your line from which his active numbers sell for $10.00-$20.00 each. He may feel that some pieces of yours are too expensive for him to buy and sell actively. Then you may wish to give him some $75.00 or $100.00 "show pieces" which you feel will lend a glamor and distinction to your display in his store. In such situations a "guaranteed" sale is permissible. That is, you would invoice him for the particular items with the written understanding that, if he does not sell them within perhaps 60 days, you will issue him credit or a refund on their return in good condition. Note that on guaranteed sales he pays freight both ways.

Your retailers may ask you to participate in some part of the cost of a special promotion they plan to do on your merchandise. Such promotional activities might include the cost of a page in a special catalog they will print and distribute or an advertisement featuring your line. The requested financial participation on the part of the producer might take the form of an additional discount on a special purchase to support such advertising, or they may request a specific sum of money representing a part of the cost of the promotion. Naturally, the additional discount, or "advertising allowance" as it is often called, is preferable to a fixed payment, since it indicates confidence on the part of the merchant in his ability to sell what he is about to promote. When you can afford such activities, these requests are common and legitimate. You must judge them on the basis of whether or not you will ultimately make a profit on the money you spend in this fashion.

Eventually you may even wish to invest part of your profits in such activities and approach the customer with such offers to encourage him to promote your wares. However, such promotion should generally take place only after your line has proven successful with a dealer, or with similar dealers in comparable areas. It should not be used as an incentive to place the line initially.

Finally, there remains the question of your policy in accepting "returns" of merchandise. Every producer must do this. Improperly packed items are damaged, defects creep into the most carefully controlled production, and catalogs and printed sales material may present an image to a particular customer which leads him to expect something other than what he receives. The good businessman stands behind his product 100% in the case of all legitimate claims, even when it hurts. However, some retailers are not legitimate and these will try to take advantage of the producer, especially if they consider him to be weak. If a buyer requests permission for a return promptly after the receipt of the goods, you should authorize the return, accept it and *inspect it to determine if his complaint was justified.* If he does this consistently, and his complaints are picayune, you will probably just stop selling him.

If he claims defects and requests a return for goods after a long period— say 90 days—you can be wary. He has probably developed the defects himself because the goods do not sell. If your buyer resold everything he bought at full price and quickly, he would be a rich man in a short time. Part of his risk is "buying wrong" and you are not obliged to accept such delayed returns from him. To insure yourself against such unjustified returns, make it a policy to refuse shipments returned unless you have given the customer authorization to return, or unless your field representatives have done so. It is always important for the small businessman to be cooperative and to bend over backward to please and service his customer. He is not expected to be a fool.

Your sales plans and policies are as much a cornerstone of your business as your product. To most creators, the time and thought required to start selling properly is a bore and a burden. However, it is necessary if you expect to establish your craft as a business. If you take the requisite time and use your intelligence and energies to do this job properly at the start, you can perhaps look forward to growing sufficiently to be able to hire others to assume these particular responsibilities. However, once in it, you may find sales work a source of excitement and a highly constructive experience.

# 7.

# Your Own Retail Store

The earliest American craftsmen made and sold their own products in the same place. In other words, they were their own retail outlet. In many respects, a craftsman is still best served by having his own store.

By selling your own product to the consumer you realize the full price of the product. When you ship to another retailer, it is probable that you will wait an average of about forty-five days before you are paid, but if you have an active shop of your own, you may well be able to convert the products you make into cash more quickly. If you can earn both the manufacturer's profit and the retailer's profit you will need to make only about half as much merchandise to earn the same total profit. You can also learn more in your own retail shop about the acceptability of your product because you, or someone working closely with you, will be in direct contact with the customer. Because of this, and for a great many other reasons, retailing should have great appeal for craftsmen either as a prime means of selling or as a supplement to wholesale selling.

Why, then, are there so few craftsmen selling through their own retail outlets? I know of relatively few craftsmen who are successfully operating their own retail outlets, and even those using shops as adjuncts to their studios and as centers for selling instruction as well as their product were few and far between. Those retail craft outlets which I observed, and many of whose owners I interviewed, have a great advantage in that the shops displayed their products to excellent advantage as well as making the craftsman secure in his control over the entire making-selling process. Perhaps the first deterrent is that few craftsmen have sufficient products of their own manufacture to stock a store and make it interesting. The work of one man, quite naturally, has a sameness about it. It is generally all of a type and would almost certainly be of a single material. In some types of craft this is quite acceptable. For example, jewelry craftsman Ed Wiener in New York City stocks his shop almost exclusively with items of his own manufacture. He makes fine gold and silver jewelry of a distinctive character in a broad price range. He is, however, in a good Madison Avenue location in the nation's biggest market and can draw from literally millions of potential customers. Thus, his shop's specialization is possible.

Similarly, when Fred Braun started his leather shop in a high traffic New York location, he put a few items in his studio window, began to sell, and broadened his line as he went along. (His customers, asking for items, often told him what to make.) He also did some custom work which increased his early business. However, unlike the case of most craft merchandise, every woman and girl is a potential customer for his sandals and other leather ready-to-wear, all of which have the happy faculty of wearing out. Perhaps if you are working in a prime, metropolitan location, you too can be highly specialized.

These exceptions notwithstanding, you may be courting trouble when you open a shop with a single type of product and especially with a limited showing of that one product. You must have enough merchandise and a sufficiently broad range of prices and appeal within that merchandise to appeal to a broad range of customers. The craftsman can, of course, join with other crafts producers to open or stock a shop. This is not at all uncommon and is often a fine idea provided the authority for management of the shop is centralized in a single individual. The craftsman can, if he has the capital to do so, also buy other merchandise to make his shop more varied. However, if you are to control your image as a craftsman, the purchased merchandise should be subordinate to your own and carefully selected to complement your own image.

Assuming you can meet the first requirement of presenting enough merchandise to sell and keep your customers interested and coming back, the second problem can well be time. Are you primarily a maker or a seller? I have seen more than one craftsman enter retailing and become so involved in the store that eventually he dropped his craft as a commercial activity and limited himself to buying and selling. However, if you prefer to regard your manufacturing as your principal activity, you will find retailing a substantial imposition on your time. A store must abide by regular retail hours, generally six days a week, and customers should be shown the courtesy and attention they deserve. The specialty merchant, such as you would be, will quickly become known for courteous service or the lack of it. The customer who has a pleasant experience when he visits your shop will praise you to others.

You are projecting a personality in your own shop. So few people have any opportunity to discuss how the things they buy and use are made that you will excite your customer's interest. Interest can result in conversation and a great deal of conversation is expensive. If you're selling a $500 fountain, you probably won't object to two hours of talk, but if it's a ten dollar bracelet a person wants, your selling time can become expensive.

In brief, then, do you have the time to open a retail shop? Apart from waiting on trade and performing the multitude of other functions that keep a retail store running, if you start to bring in other merchandise you will need buying time to seek it out in addition to all of your other activities. This adds up to long hours and lots of work.

Lots of people are willing to work, but not every hard-working retailer makes a go of it. In 1966 Dun and Bradstreet reported over 6,000 retail failures, far more than in manufacturing or other types of business. And it is impossible to know how many shops just tried it and closed up without actually declaring bankruptcy. It is perhaps because the retail store is so familiar to all of us that we think it would be a simple thing to manage one. While the retail establishment does have decided advantages for you, as a craftsman, it is not without risk.

Since no two craft retail establishments are really alike, and since they may be of dominant or subordinate importance in the craftsman's marketing activity, it will be profitable to stop briefly to take a quick look at two quite different but successful manufacturer/retailer craft situations.

Potter David Gil of Bennington, Vermont is one of the craftsmen who has amply demonstrated his ability to create, produce and sell. When asked why he opened his first retail operation, a stand on the highway open during the summer tourist months, he answered, "It was an act of desperation. We needed the money to live on and in those days I wasn't yet wholesaling very successfully." While today his pottery business is approaching half a million dollars annual volume, of which about 30% comes out of his retail shops, it wasn't always so. "A good day was $30 on the highway, but it was $30!" He continued, "When things were really tight, it helped. And it opened my eyes. Almost every day we sold something." I remember that stand, and the overhead was very low.

A couple of years later he decided to consolidate the retail shop with the pottery, and he hung up a sign at the pottery and another near the center of town. The retail business continued to grow as did his wholesale business which is still handled by his sales agent, Richards Morgenthau Company in New York. At this point, with increased production, the shop took on another kind of importance. It became a good outlet for his "seconds," test items, and discontinued merchandise. These could not be shipped to his wholesale customers. "Even today, about 80% of our retail business is in seconds," he reported. He sells his off-selection goods at a discount of 50% from retail, thereby getting as much for his seconds as for his first quality merchandise sold at wholesale. As his production has grown better and as more capable equipment has been purchased, the ratio of seconds to perfect merchandise has dropped, but there are still enough goods to create a costly problem had he not developed the means of disposing of them.

While the wholesale business still predominates at Bennington Potters, Mr. Gil finds no conflict in selling both wholesale and retail. "I feel that all exposure for my product is good exposure," he will tell you. If a wholesale account buys in his factory outlet shop, his agent receives credit and the account, having made contact with the source of the merchandise and its maker, has a new interest in the line. Conversely, customers who have bought Bennington Pottery in their local retail shops and, as a result, seek him out when they are in Bennington, will probably "save" by buying a few seconds at the factory store, but they will return home with a renewed interest in the merchandise and speak to their friends about the pottery when they use it. The hometown retailer wins too. Of course, Gil's retail shop in Bennington and his newer one in Rockport, Massachusetts do not compete with any of his important customers. A craftsman working in Chicago, for example, might well have to make a choice between selling Marshall Field & Company, and selling from his own store.

An interesting observation was offered to me at Bennington in regard to a craftsman's shop buying lines which he does not make. "First," David Gil remembered, "we started to buy component parts made outside for our own pottery, a wood handle or tray. At that time we needed all available capital to improve our plant and equipment. Production came first then, as now," he added. "We now have some funds to buy other lines of wood, glass and so on, to offer in our shops and it does make them more interesting." The things he has selected to sell, I must add, are in superb taste, ranging from knitted Peruvian ski ponchos to American hand-blown stemware. He has also, with the expansion of his Bennington retail store, begun to show the work of other local craftsmen and sell it: hand-loomed wool, leather goods, printed silks, etc. He is, in effect, becoming a local craft center.

Like most younger craftsmen, when the Gils started they had close contacts with their customers and could establish the close personal relationships through which most of their accounts still know them. As they grew it became more difficult, but they still try. David is proud that the customer coming to his shop to buy is still offered a cup of coffee, and tourists can, once a day, go on a tour of the pottery. "Once, not very long ago, we really couldn't afford such niceties or the few hours of manpower that the interruption of a tour would cost." When asked what advice he would give to a craftsman just starting in retail, Mr. Gil made a number of points: "A shop must have one or more staple articles for which it is known and for which customers will come back. Our trigger mug and dinnerware starter sets are the prime keys to our repeat business. Then, we try to build the unit sale. A dinner plate sale at $1.50 retail is nice, but a starter set at $10 is nicer. Rather than offering our off-selection mugs at 50¢ each, we try to build the sale by giving our customers a set of twelve for $5. Time spent with customers unnecessarily is expensive. While we train our girls to serve the customer, we've set up the shop to be as much of a self-service operation as possible."

In addition to an active wholesale and an important retail business, the Gils have begun to use their own customer list profitably for a very limited mail order effort. They mail, at this time, only to people who have bought from them or registered at the store. Happily, they are not now actively exploiting very many secondary channels of sale because they have everything they can do to meet the current demand for their excellent products.

The business activities of leather craftsman Fred Braun are as different from the Gil's business as Bennington is from New York City. Mr. Braun opened his first retail shop in Greenwich Village in 1952 with $300 capital. (I've yet to meet a craftsman who started with an open checkbook in his hand.) His bustling workshop and showroom in New York now services four of his own stores in New York plus a thriving wholesale business. Unlike David Gil, he feels that retailing is the prime outlet for his work and he treats wholesale selling as a secondary, if important, plus business. He intends to keep it that way since he feels retailing gives him greater control over his destinies.

With the help of his wife and associates, he still makes everything he sells, and his employees number over 100. When one talks to Mr. Braun, it all seems as simple as just opening a shop, but as you get further into discussions, it becomes quite apparent that he is a sound businessman with a real merchandising sense and drive. Above all, it's quite apparent that his retail business took, and still takes, a lot of work.

When asked why he has chosen the direct retail method of selling his products, Mr. Braun said, "I didn't have enough capital to do anything else. I made a pair of sandals, put them in the window and sold them. I used the money to buy more material to make more goods. In retail, your money turns over rapidly." He still maintains the same sort of attitude toward his turnover rate and reports that his stores turn their inventory about ten times per year.

A "turn of inventory" is a key consideration in retailing and justifies a short digression at this point. It means that if a store averages $1,000 in stock on hand and it turns over its stock ten times a year, it will do a gross volume of $10,000 per year. This does not mean, of course, that every item in the group will be stocked and sold ten times. Some goods may turn over 25 times and others, once. The ones that only turn-over a few times are less profitable and should generally be examined to see if they cannot be improved or replaced. Most stores would envy Fred Braun's rapid turnover rate. In 1966 a craft shop in Alexandria, Virginia reported less than a three-time turnover in the first eight months of operation, and during the same period a craft jeweler in New York said that he averaged a turnover rate of approximately seven times.

The number of times each year that you can convert your inventory into cash and back into retail inventory is critical as a measure of your potential profit. Let us assume you make a 15% *retail* profit on your sales and start with a hypothetical $1,000. Each time you sell $1,000 you make $150. Obviously, the more frequently you can do it, the more money you will make on your investment and the work embodied in it. There's an old saying in business that the cheapest "bath" you take is the one you take quickly. In other words, if you know that certain goods aren't moving, close them out for what you can get for them and reinvest the money in things which will resell. Braun's outstanding conviction seemed to be that a good product is the basis of a good business. "We make a good product. That brings us our customers," he said. "It is our best advertising." In fact he does no other advertising for fear of increasing the cost of his product. Most successful craftsmen I have met voiced similar sentiments and, I believe, demonstrated their statement in their product. Fred Braun flies in the face of modern merchandising practice in another respect. "If you offer your customer credit," he stated, "they may buy the credit and not the product. Then I can't be sure if my product is right." He offers no credit. He has devoted his energies to making a product superior to the commercial goods available and feels that this month's product and customer will bring next month's.

Braun insists that he must make two profits, as you should, and carefully controls his business toward that end. "The craftsman making his own goods and selling them should make the manufacturer's profit plus the seller's profit." It takes some thoughtful accounting to know that you are doing this, but Braun goes so far as to set up each store on a separate account so that he can tell exactly how everything is doing. Depending on where you are located and on the nature of your craft, your producing unit and your selling unit can often be contiguous so that your management time can be shared between both situations. In this way the value of your own retail outlet in testing new goods will be greatly enhanced.

Like David Gil, Braun is production-minded. Concentrating in leather only, he has purchased some basic leather-working machinery, and he employs artisans from many parts of the world to help him. He works only from select leathers and still dyes and stains them in his own shop. In walking through his now substantial factory, Mrs. Braun made it a point to show me that many, many hand operations are retained to insure the craft quality and craft character of his work.

His line is, by commercial standards, a relatively limited one. It includes footwear for both men and women, as well as women's bags and leather coats. However, this line covers a price range of $10 to over $100 per item at retail, giving him a broad range of economic and age appeal. He has concentrated on what Mrs. Braun characterized as "the casual woman," since fewer style changes are required by this group than in the high fashion field. Both the limitation of product and the limitation of style change tend toward substantial production efficiency.

In his wholesale activity he sells to department stores at the same price at which he delivers goods to his own outlets. Where his own stores in the metropolitan New York area compete with outlets to which he wholesales, identical retail prices are held by agreement.

Craftsmen like those mentioned above have proven that a good living can be made in the crafts. David Gil, Fred Braun, and Ed Weiner did not start as large, well-financed manufacturers or retailers. They started with an absolute minimum of help, both making and selling their products themselves. They have all proven that retailing can be an important source of income and Gil and Braun are both wholesaling and retailing successfully. They have proven, as have many others, that it is possible to develop both a mastery of a craft and of its merchandising. Such shops are building a fine image for the professional craftsman and should prove encouraging to newer craft merchants.

The proprietor of a top craft shop in New York, who also had several years of experience in commercial real estate, stated that in renting a store, "You get exactly what you pay for." The fact that the Gils located in an out of the way part of a limited market town probably has something to do with the fact that their retail business remained incidental for a number of years. Ed Wiener, speaking of his newly opened shop, said, "We located where our customers live and shop. It's not a question of traffic alone, but of the right kind of traffic. The people who see your shop must be the kind that are sympathetic to what you do." Location is tremendously important, especially with a limited advertising budget or none at all, and a very reputable agent, or several, should be called upon to advise you before you sign a lease for a shop.

Location also brings up the question of the price range of the merchandise which you offer for sale. The Greenwhich Village craftsman often depends on price. He has a lot of traffic and it's often not particularly affluent. A young avant-garde group is likely to be his principal source of customers. Consequently, most village shops have a broad range of lower-priced goods. Ron Pearson's Shop I in Rochester, N.Y., has some impulse merchandise, but one would judge by studying his goods that he has developed a significant clientele for better things at higher prices. Most shops report that the majority of their customers will travel to get to them, meaning that the customer does not necessarily live in the immediate trading area. However, the first time a customer passes you she must be drawn in by the look of your shop before she can be sold.

Both expensive and impulse merchandise will be needed in a retail shop. If you, as a merchant, have only one and two dollar sales, and unless you can make a great many sales each day, you'll fail to make money. The larger sales are necessary to profit. Conversely, as one experienced shop keeper told me, "The low-priced item traps the browser. I don't mind making a small sale if the item is good because the customer is going to take home a constant reminder that I'm here." Many people will not enter a store unless they feel they can purchase some small item. They may be curious about your shop but afraid to spend time there and walk out empty-handed. Knowing they can pick up some little thing allows them to browse relaxedly.

In display, as in most other arts, a change of pace is important. One small craft shop I visited in New York showed the work of three individuals in wood, weaving and pottery. As a result of being together, and each quite different, there was a change of rhythm and mood in each display in the store. Any one of the collections alone might well have become quite monotonous. If you are working in one material and cannot interest other craftsmen in setting up a shop with you, you can achieve a varied display by changing backgrounds and other settings frequently. If you have pottery and limit yourself to a relatively few textures and glazes, some of your things displayed on fabric will look quite different from others placed on glass shelves. A weathered branch used as a display prop to lift some items off a flat plane can make them much more interesting than if all pieces were placed on flat tables or shelves. Placing merchandise in a table of sand raked into interesting patterns can be as effective as the most expensive commercial display case. Esthetic imagination and a willingness to experiment are the key ingredients in a well displayed shop.

One rule to remember in display is that display is the art of creating backgrounds which will show off the product to advantage. Your backgrounds and props should never overpower the product you are showing. If they are to be examined close at hand, they can be subtle and intricate. If they are to be viewed from a distance—across a street, perhaps—they must be striking to attract interest but also serve to show your merchandise well when examined more closely.

Displays are perishable. If your average customer is likely to drop by your shop every three weeks, then you should schedule a change of display in one prominent part of the shop at least every three weeks. Seasonal themes can often lend an air of interest to a retail establishment even though the theme has little to do with the merchandise offered. The major holidays, changes of season, well publicized local or national events and other happenings which capture general interest can all be sources of display inspiration.

Small, commonplace and inexpensive props used in display can suggest possible uses for your products. A glass jar filled with colorful soap balls can suggest its use as a decorative accessory for the bath. If candy is put in it, your customer may visualize it in a living room or kitchen setting, whereas filled with pretzels or chips it might suggest bar use. A unique design for a serving dish may not be recognizable unless it is actually shown in use. All sorts of artificial food products for display use are available through standard display materials outlets, as are many other useful accessories to help show your product. Often a collection of dried stalks and grasses, or interesting rocks collected nearby, will serve you as well.

The judicious use of lighting can make or break the effect of a presentation. If you are showing a roughly textured piece, a harsh, directional light will accent the texture. Daylight in a window may tend to subdue it and lessen the impact of your wares. With a few inexpensive gelatin filters you can also introduce color into backgrounds or vary the intensity of colors of merchandise shown. An early investment in a few reflector floods and spot lamps can add measurably to the effectiveness of your presentation for many months to come.

While the simple job of housekeeping in your store may seem quite unromantic, it is probably more important than the most creative of displays. A clean, shining, well cared for display of merchandise is a must. The way you treat your goods will immediately communicate an attitude to your customer. He will unconsciously feel that a bright and spotless display indicates that the items are valued by you, the owner, whereas soiled and dusty samples reflect little regard on your part and should not be considered as articles of value by him. A bucket, a sponge, and a rag are probably as important as any display materials you are ever likely to find. Only a closeout or seconds operation can afford less than a spotless appearance.

While several items which will establish character and mood for your store should be displayed importantly and with plenty of "air" around them, don't hesitate to crowd or group others. In a craft shop, as in an antique shop, most customers will wish to browse and make their own discovery. A shop which makes everything very available may tend to eliminate pockets of mystery and thereby lessen a customer's interest. If you have a group shop or a large store, this will be less true than if you have a small store with a rather restricted line.

Finally, as a general rule, articles should be clearly marked with price. A customer will often have a specific price range in mind when she enters your shop. If the first article she likes is substantially higher in price than she feels she can afford, your customer may be inhibited from searching further. If all prices are marked the customer can seek out an item in his range without embarrassment.

When I solicited display advice from one craftsman whose shop was most exciting, he could only tell me, "You just have to do what comes naturally." As a craftsman you most probably have a highly developed ability to visualize in terms of the products you make. It takes only a disciplining of this innate ability to see with your mind's eye what you wish to create to allow you to work effectively in displaying your merchandise.

In order to keep a shop interesting, new things should be added frequently. The freshness of the inventory is just as important as its quality. When you begin work on new products, put a few out to test them. Put them where they will surely be seen, but try not to lead customers to them. You will soon see if they are attracting interest and are likely to sell. If they move out, you have a directive to expand the line quickly. If they do not, try to determine why they are not moving and, if possible, try to correct their deficiencies. If you can't sell them well, get them off display or close them out.

In determining what merchandise should be most importantly displayed in breadth, there is only one criterion; will it pay for the good space it occupies? New developments are a necessary part of growth in both the crafts and business. Experiments must be exposed, and you must be guided in stocking your shop by the *buying* reaction you receive to their exposure.

In talking with merchants, one thing that comes through is that each believes that he is different. The successful ones usually are. One who could lay claim to success, and a very fast success after he opened four years ago, credited his good fortune not only to good display of interesting goods, but also to the hours the store keeps. The following example shows what intelligent interest in a shop's results can prove. Buyways calculates that their average sale is about $15. However, the average unit sale goes up significantly later in the day. They further noted that while the percentage of customers in their shop during a given day was heavily in favor of women, men were better craft customers for better merchandise. Arlene Shotz, one of Buyways' owners, reported, "Men seem to have a greater respect for the work of human hands and a greater affinity for most art crafts." Seldom was a sale of $100 made without a man present. Men, of course, are generally free to shop only in the evening. Buyways stayed open until 11:00 P.M. or later and showed a profit in their first quarter of operation! You must adapt yourself to your customer's pattern instead of expecting him to conform to your convenience in retailing.

Learning to sell in a retail shop can be difficult enough if you've never done it before, but learning to sell your own work properly is even harder. You must try to see your things as your customer wishes to see them, and not as you would like to have her see them. You will, quite naturally, see the piece in terms of what went into it and its artistic merits. Unless your customer is deeply interested in your craft, she could not care less about the techniques that produced it. The average purchaser buys something because of what he thinks it will do for him. Don't involve him in your concerns. Try to sense what his reactions are. A bit of small talk when your customer is ready can often make the sale by giving you a clue as to what the customer wants. Start talking to the customer in his terms. If he has shown interest in a stoneware bowl, tell him about its use as a centerpiece, for fruit, the fact that she can cook in it, and that it comes in a range of colors to match any interior. These points may be important to the customer. It is his point of view that will sell it to him, not yours. And suggest the matching candlesticks to go with it. The real estate salesman who marches you through a dozen depressing houses saying, "And this is *your* living room opening on a lovely terrace for *your* summer parties; from here you can see the school for *your* children," may make a dismal effect when the shoe doesn't fit, but the technique can certainly sell things when the customer really imagines himself on that terrace or dangling those gold earrings at a party.

While the general subject of pricing is covered elsewhere, it can be noted here that retailers in the craft fields generally take a markup of approximately 100% on cost. This does not mean double your direct manufacturing cost. You must first calculate your manufacturer's selling price, a price at which you could profitably sell your product to somebody else. Sell it to your own store, on the books, at the same price. Your store should then double the price to retail. Most stores interviewed for this text reported taking a gross profit of only 33% to 40% of retail on such pieces as might be considered fine art, and it was not uncommon for few-of-a-kind items to be priced over double cost when visual value appeared to sustain a higher price.

When figuring retail costs for your products, it is dangerous to price on the basis of a first piece cost. The second piece will take less time and thus cost less, and you stand a chance of pricing yourself out of the market. Price on an estimated production cost allowing for production economies.

A store, like any other business, requires administrative controls. The cost of doing business should be carefully recorded. It should not be considered as one with your manufacturing costs since you could be ahead on one phase of your activity and losing on another without knowing where to correct the trouble. Inventories are among the most important of the retailer's controls and must be made at least every six months, preferably each quarter. If possible, you should try to keep a perpetual inventory, noting goods as they are added to stock and as they are sold, so that you always have an approximate idea of your inventory value. Without inventory controls you may think you're losing money, only to find that you've been putting it all back into merchandise and are in a heavy inventory position. The box can be full of cash at night, and you may well be drawing out money at the expense of your total net worth by depleting inventory while you are actually losing money on the shop.

Many costs enter into the operation of a retail business even if that business is a simple one. Different proprietors or accounts may name expenses in different ways or group them differently, but basically the expenditures will be of a similar nature in any retail store. The following categories of income and expenditure listed as they might be found on a retail store's balance sheet can serve as a guide from which you can develop your own form:

NET SALES:
(from which all the following are deducted)
Sales and administrative payroll
Rental on property
Advertising
Publicity
Sales equipment
Freight, express and parcel post
Taxes
Supplies
Display materials
Services purchased (might include accounting, legal fees, etc.)
Insurance
Telephone/telegraph
Depreciation and amortization (of fixtures, cash registers, etc.)
Travel and transportation
Bad debt losses (bad checks as well as uncollectable debts)
Misc. unclassified

From the balance left, after the above items are deducted from net sales, you must still allow for payment of federal taxes and local taxes as they apply to your particular area and business.

By periodically checking how you are spending your money, you can tell where you can most easily effect economies in your operation. A quarterly check using a balance sheet form similar to the above can tell you how your business is going from a financial point of view and help you catch negative implications early. Remember that volume is worthless if it cannot be profitable.

Finally, while some retail shops can turn a profit in the first few months, most take a year or more. Surely you can hope to draw some semblance of a paycheck for your own labor before you show a profit, but that will be a payment for your time and will require your time. A conservative accountant, even one who felt your idea for a shop to be valid, would probably caution you to go into retailing only if you can afford to equip your store and carry it for six months to a year without a significant profit. Examine your own situation realistically and get some professional help on projecting your costs of operating a retail business; then, if it looks solid, go ahead. As one friend told me, "A person who's willing to work at both making and selling can make a darned good living in the crafts." He knows because he's doing it. Perhaps retailing can work for you too.

# 8.

# Mail Order Selling

The number of small ads appearing regularly in consumer publications, and especially in the "shelter books," attests to the fact that the small firm can sell effectively by mail. Conversely, the number of once-and-only-once advertisers who lose $500 or more on a one-time mail order trial each year indicates the need for an intelligent and considered approach to the mail-order market.

Experienced and successful mail-order merchants in the specialty item field agree that it costs more to sell mail order than to sell through standard wholesale or retail channels, and that the risks may well be considerably higher. Mr. George Howard, who heads Jeff Elliot Craftsman, and whose success in this and other mail-order enterprises has made him one of the leaders in the specialty mail-order field, quotes a direct sales cost of about 35% of retail to sell by mail. This figure is drawn from a business which is established and has a great many years of experience in the field. His costs consist importantly of advertising space, ad and catalog preparation, postage, and of course, normal operating overhead. Since a product cannot be sold for more on a mail-order offering than it would bring through a retailer, 15% remains to cover other costs and profits (including the cost of merchandise which doesn't sell), or perhaps 25% if you consider another 10% of retail which would normally be paid as a wholesale sales commission. Mr. Howard states that his preference for mail order is based upon many factors. No expensive fixed rental for a retail location is required, and he can work with a relatively short line of goods compared to that which would be needed to make a retail operation profitable. He observes that selling craft items at retail takes a great deal of time on the part of the retail salespersons involved, another hidden cost which he need not contend with.

Other merchants in the craft field found mail order a profitable supplementary means of marketing in addition to wholesale and retail selling. One risk in selling mail order exclusively is that you don't have a second chance to sell your goods. If you offer an item in a retail shop at ten dollars as your normal price, and you find it does not sell, chances are pretty good that you can reduce the price and sell it at either a reduced profit or a small loss. In mail-order selling, if you have prepared even a minimum stock to cover an ad and the ad does not "pull," you are stuck with the goods. Thus mail order, as we shall examine it below, is recommended for the craftsman only as a possible supplementary marketing channel, and not as a basic means of making his sales.

The risks in mail order can be high. First, there is the cost of the ad which will vary from one publication to another, but which can be conservatively set at a minimum of about $500 per ad. A top mail-order merchandiser has said that it is a very good ad that will bring in 400% of cost.

That is to say that if you invest $500 in the ad, and you book $2,000 worth of business as a result of it, this will be a pleasant exception. In this happy instance, the normal wholesale value of the goods you sold at $2,000 would be between $800 and $1,000. On a highly successful advertisement your gross profits will approximate 25%. Before all the discouraging facts are placed on the table it must be said that the business is obviously profitable, and these figures are stated only to make a newcomer to the field aware of the risks. On the average, as you would expect, the ads pay for themselves. This is not to say that any given ad may not prove to be a losing proposition, and that you should not enter mail-order merchandising unless you can realistically withstand the loss. Ads pay off for the mail-order houses most importantly through giving them the names of active mail-order buyers for their mailing lists. These are used subsequently to product profitable sales through a catalog follow up.

There is always the possibility of a free editorial in the shopping column of one of the magazines with a substantial mail order "pull." If you can convince a shopping column editor that you do have a good item and can excite her interest in it, the editor may cooperate and include your item in her shopping column presentation. This is especially true if you can talk her into using her column to "test" the publication for its potential in selling your products.

This will become easier after you have run your first mail-order ads and can show your published efforts to an editor. At that point she'll be more likely to believe you're serious about mail-order selling. If you can't see an editor, publicity information and pictures mailed to her will have to suffice. However, if at all possible, you should get to know your shopping editors personally. As a craftsman, you have a good chance of exciting editorial interest with a unique product.

What type of merchandise will mail order best? As a quick review of the magazines will tell you, it should be merchandise which is not generally available at retail. The large rural market which built the mail-order giants such as Sears is, in large measure, now within reach of adequate retail shopping. Even the farmer can buy his staple requirements without recourse to mail order. If your item is unusual, it should not be an item that needs explaining. Its function must be fairly obvious. Readers browsing through a magazine will not tolerate involved presentations and there is little space for them in mail-order ads.

Your mail-order "salesman" will be a black and white photograph. An item that depends on color, texture, or detail is inappropriate for mail-order ads. Even though such an item may prove most attractive at retail when sold over the counter, it may fail in a mail-order presentation. The mail-order item must be obvious in its function and sell on shape and form. Further, the item which has a story—something unique in its character or background—is a good mail-order prospect. Can your selected item be made interesting in a few words?

Mail-order operators disagree widely on the price range that will sell most actively. While, statistically, items in the $5 or $10 range are favored, a number of successful mail merchandisers say that price is secondary if the item has the appearance of good value. Naturally, a higher unit sale, the sale of a more expensive item, is desirable from the standpoint of immediate profits, since you'll probably expend the same effort on wrapping, addressing, record keeping and shipping for a low priced item than you will for a higher priced unit. However, if you're building a list of mail-order buyers, more readers will respond to a lower priced offering. In fact, such low priced units are frequently referred to as "list builders." Once you have hit upon a successful mail-order item, in addition to placing it in publications other than the one in which it first appeared, you should immediately make plans to follow it up with similar merchandise. Co-ordinated units can prove as successful as your first "hit."

Freight can be a key factor in mail-order merchandising. As you will note from a review of mail-order ads, most companies offer merchandise prepaid. Obviously, then, the cost of shipping an item must be considered in judging its profitability. Similarly, it must be an item which will ship safely. Excessive calls for replacement of broken goods can quickly turn a good seller into an expensive nightmare.

If your item is too large or heavy for economical parcel post shipment, there is adequate precedent for shipping freight collect. Firms which specialize in selling larger items report that while "freight collect" in an ad may be a deterrent, it is seldom fatal to an offer's success.

Perhaps from your point of view as a craftsman, the most important feature of your article is that it represent you as you wish to be seen. Your image will be riding on those first ads. Their prime purpose is to establish you as a source of merchandise of a distinctive and desirable character. Your follow through on mail-order service will establish your reliability.

Next we come to the ad itself. It cannot be overemphasized that the preparation and placing of mail order advertising is no job for the amateur. You will need an ad agency, and more importantly, you will need an agency that specializes successfully in the mail-order business. The publications which run the ads can often help in referring you to such firms, and agencies generally have a directory which will tell you what agency prepared and placed advertising for a firm whose ads particularly appeal to you. The 15% of space cost plus production charges that ad agencies earn is a good investment. Even the long-experienced mail-order houses recognize their reliance on professional agency help.

A few guides to working with your agency will perhaps prove helpful. George Howard warns that the craftsman who has a limited mail-order budget to risk had better choose the very best—which generally means expensive—medium for one ad rather than going into two ads in less productive books. When you make your photo for the ad, keep it simple. Your photo should be functional and show the product clearly. Resist the temptation to make a great, "arty" shot. Like the photo, the layout of your ad should be clear and expository. If the price is low, feature it. If it's high, bury it in body copy. A provocative headline that will stop somebody long enough to read the body copy is vital. The body copy should be succinct and should call for a purchase. Lots of words don't necessarily sell. Your sales pitch must be delivered completely in as few words as possible.

The best ad will not pull heavily if it is in the wrong place or published at the wrong time. For craftsmen, the shelter publications are prime media, i.e., *House and Garden, House Beautiful, American Home,* etc. There may be other good presentation mediums depending on your product. If you're making an unusual travel purse, *Holiday* might be a book to consider. *When* being as important as *where,* you would be well-advised to make your first trial in November, December, or October (in that order of choice), or second best, in the spring months of February or March. The cost of an ad is the same at all seasons, and these months are the most productive for mail order. Remember that a December issue probably hits the newsstands in November, etc. Dating of issue publications varies somewhat from one magazine to another. While the publications carry the heaviest mail-order advertising during these peak periods, and your ad will thus have more competition in these "heavy" issues, experience shows that these months are the most productive for advertisers.

We have suggested that a program of advertising, alone, is not likely to be profitable for the mail-order craftsman, and have then proceeded to examine the ad. How then can it be profitable? Profits in mail order, according to most practitioners, are made on follow ups and second sales. If an ad pulls inquiries and orders sufficient to cover the cost of the ad, most firms would consider it reasonably successful. Once a consumer has responded to your advertisement sufficiently to send you a request for more information or an order, he is a likely prospect for your other merchandise. On your mailing list he is of value. Thus, while a catalog is not mandatory for mail order, it will very likely mean the difference between a good profit and a small one.

A catalog has a number of advantages over the small ad which brings you your first response. It can show things in more detail, and it can show more things. A prospect may find your style attractive, but the particular item shown may not prove sufficiently attractive to call forth an order. Your catalog gives you a second chance to pick up that order. A line in your ad requesting that the reader write you for your free catalog is often the most important part of your ad.

A catalog, like a good retail store, must offer a wide selection of merchandise in most instances and cover a fairly broad price range. The variety of merchandise is also a key to its success. While a catalog showing personal leather goods can be profitable, a catalog showing leather goods plus jewelry, plus perhaps some handwoven ready to wear merchandise, would have a better chance of success. Remember that each catalog costs money and can only be profitable if there is something in it which a reasonable number of people will buy.

If properly designed and produced a larger catalog showing more merchandise may cost no more to mail than a thinner book. (Before you prepare your final catalog with your printer, check your local postmaster to make sure your book will mail at the minimum rate. His suggestions can often save you a lot of money.) With a broader presentation in view, the idea of combining your catalog and mail-order efforts with one or more local craftsmen other than yourself may make sense. By a joint effort costs can be reduced and a greater variety and potential sale can be presented in your catalog.

If you are both wholesaling and mail ordering, a single catalog with a separate wholesale terms and conditions sheet may serve both purposes. The language and presentation of such a dual purpose catalog should be suited to mail order, however, as the professional language and economy of a wholesale catalog is usually not prepared to excite the consumer to buy, whereas good mail-order copy which contains all vital information can do a wholesale job reasonably well. The effectiveness of your mail-order catalog will depend to a great degree on who receives it. Ideally, every prospective customer should have expressed interest in your product, although this is seldom practicable. Expressions of interest will have come through the mail-order ads. If you are also retailing, you should keep a register and ask each visitor to your shop to enter his name and address. In this fashion you will build your own list over a period of time. The lists you build yourself will actually be the most profitable. In addition, it will probably be necessary for you to obtain other lists to make an economical catalog mailing. The basic preparation cost of a catalog is the same whether you print 100 or 100,000. Paper and press time cost more, but in greater quantity the unit cost of printed matter drops markedly, and your profits, given good lists, will climb as your print quantity increases. Mail order firms will generally not even test mail a list with less than 5,000 books, and most consider an economical mailing to be upwards of 25,000. However, if your catalog is not too expensive, perhaps 10,000 would be a workable test for you.

Since it will take you quite a while to accumulate your own list of a size for economical mailing, there are several ways to obtain additional lists. You can offer to exchange lists with another mail order merchant seeking a market similar to your own. List brokers can often find you a suitable list which you can rent or buy already prepared on labels. The cost of such rented lists is generally about $20 per thousand. The key to the list value is quality. Is it fresh, i.e. are addresses current? Is it a list that will reach a market likely to buy from you? Further, is it a list which has been prepared to include only active mail-order buyers? A good list broker or personal contact with a firm which is mail ordering a non-competitive item can often answer many of these questions, but only a test with your own catalog will truly tell you what you have bought. A test is simply limited mailing to a representative sample of your customer list. Too small a sample will tell you little, as a couple of good orders will throw it off. If you test on 10% of a purchased list, i.e. a minimum of 2,500 pieces, you can begin to get some reasonable idea of the list's value. Simultaneously, test it against your own list with another 2,500. Even a limited quantity of a small catalog mailed to your own customer list can often prove profitable because your list "quality" will be high and a high percentage of response can be expected.

While the evaluation of a list response can be a highly technical job, you can get a good idea by checking a few points. First, what percentage of people to whom you mail will respond with orders? While the profitable level depends on the cost of your mailing and the size of each order, a response of less than 1% would undoubtedly be unsatisfactory. A response of 5% would generally be considered phenomenal for an "outside" list. By projecting the percentage of response and multiplying it by the average size of your order, you will get an idea of the dollar volume per thousand of catalogs mailed. Knowing the cost of mailing a thousand catalogs, you will then be able to relate your efforts to potential profitability. While mail order can perhaps make a profit on ads alone, the risk is high and profits are necessarily limited. For instance, if an ad doesn't pull, you have no recourse to sell your goods. A catalog gives you another chance to present your goods again and differently. In order to develop a real mail-order business, a catalog is almost vital. This is so true that many mail-order houses which have been highly successful treat their advertising primarily as a means of obtaining names for their catalog mailing list. A serious entry into the mail-order field without plans to produce a catalog, and a substantial catalog of at least 16 pages, should not be seriously considered.

Whether you are considering advertisements or a catalog, there are certain general statements which can apply to your activity.

While no guarantee need be stated, it is preferable to announce that you offer a satisfaction guarantee. This means that if a customer is not satisfied, for any reason, you will refund the purchase price of the merchandise. The number of returns received by most mail-order houses are very few and most report no special problem in this regard. Remember that your customer does not know you. He may have confidence in the publication presenting your ad, but you are an unknown quantity to the buyer. The guarantee is a means of building confidence. A rule of decency and reason must prevail on accepting returns. If, for example, a customer returned an item that had obviously been used for a long period or abused, you are not obliged to be stupid about allowing the return. However, in mail order more than in any other type of retail business, you must work on the assumption that the customer is right and use every means to sustain customer confidence.

In closing this brief discussion of mail-order activity, the one point that must be stressed as important above everything is record keeping. From the date of your first effort every detail of your successes and failures must be recorded in a retrievable form. When you run an ad you must key it. The general method is to include a department number. For example, "write to department A-6" may mean to you that "A" for December tells you when the ad was run, and 6 designates *True Magazine.* You will then begin to learn what publications pulled best for you and what months were most remunerative.

Similarly, by identifying each advertisement you can begin to analyze the character of the presentation that produces the best response. Also, the order blank included as part of your catalog should indicate which list it was mailed against. Thus, when your order is received you can begin to develop comparative records of which lists pulled for you. Knowing when a list was mailed will also be important in your calculations of inventory. Mail orders must be shipped promptly if you are to avoid a welter of paper work answering inquiries and repairing customer confidence, if that is possible. While mail-order response lags will differ from house to house, Mrs. Arlene Shotz of Buyways in New York reports that if you multiply the response received during the first week after an ad breaks by $3\frac{1}{2}$, you will have a fair prediction of total sales on the ad. With your merchandise the response may be different, but only a good record keeping system will tell you. As in all marketing undertakings, a careful observation of what successful firms in the field are doing will be your best text, and experience can be your best teacher. An active mail-order business can bring you wholesale inquiries and excite customers to visit your store. Each area of selling activity can strengthen the others, and mail order, if your product is right and you are ready to gamble, can be a plus volume of significant value to the craftsman.

# 9.

## Some Specialized Markets for the Craftsman

Most of us tend to think about markets in terms of our own buying patterns and habits. There are other, sometimes almost hidden, markets which we are not aware of as consumers and which can move a great deal of merchandise profitably and easily. Some of these are especially well-suited to the craft producer.

Ideally, the specialized market for the craftsman's product would be a limited volume market which could pay a higher price for a product with unique quality and character. In markets which demand short runs in terms of industrial production, and which wish to customize or individualize the product, the craftsman should be able to compete very favorably.

THE INSTITUTIONAL MARKET

The contract or institutional market, as it is sometimes called, exhibits exactly these characteristics. Hotels, motels, restaurants, colleges, clubs, steamship companies, corporation offices, and often religious institutions, are all a part of this potential market. The largest of these, desiring to furnish quarters with individualized products in order to establish an identity, represents such a tiny market for a production factory that tooling becomes excessive and production profitable only at extremely high prices. A limited production run with low tooling is called for. Enter the craftsman.

Since individualization for this market presupposes that the institution buying goods wants to project its own image or personality through a special article, you have another advantage as the designer-producer. You can determine, yourself, exactly what your buyer wants and make it for him under your own supervision. His ideas, as supplemented by yours, will not suffer in translation through a large organization. This can be crucial in making the sale.

Since the short runs are the *modus operandi* of the crafts, you should be able to produce profitably at a reasonable price. The contract buyer expects to pay more for made-to-order items than for goods which are mass produced. Perhaps some of your standard items, with a minimum of adaptation, can be made to serve the contract buyer's needs. Even your standard items will be relatively unique and distinctive when compared to widely distributed, factory-produced merchandise. A famous New York restaurateur pays a Vermont potter 50¢ for a mug when he could easily buy a bar glass for a dime. However, this special container makes it possible for him to charge a bit more for an exotic drink, and the dozens of mugs that are "adopted" by the establishment's customers more than repay him in word-of-mouth advertising.

Your demonstrated ability to design a distinctive product is probably your most powerful sales tool in this market. While the majority of institutions are purchasing clean, contemporary furnishings and accessories because of the functional demands made on their equipment, there are as many variations of taste and design theme as there are establishments. Each installation tries to develop its own distinctive look and character and you will generally be more successful if you study the existing ambience and try to adapt your work to it rather than trying to impose your taste on the buyer.

Lee Jaffee, vice-president in charge of creative purchasing for Restaurant Associates, a group operating many of New York's most glamorous and interesting restaurants, stated, "We went to the manufacturers of standard institutional products, but they didn't have anything for us. In trying to create the image we had envisioned for each establishment, we had no place to go but directly to the craftsman. We're creating a show and our customers enjoy it. Food without atmosphere would not be as interesting, and it has paid off in profits." Profits are what the restauranteur, the hotel keeper, and others are looking for. Restaurant Associates, working with craftsmen, has provided many examples of what imaginative attention to details can do for institutional equipment and furnishings.

Try to determine what the "feel" of an installation is, and note the predominant colors and textures used before you attempt to develop a product for an institution's use. The character of your product should complement and re-emphasize the character of the establishment as a whole. It must make its design statement in the ambience of the total design statement.

Design is important in another respect; one new idea can frequently sell an entire job.

A craft furniture producer, for example, cannot compete with a Southern furniture plant in providing a motel with fifty chests of drawers. However, if the craftsman will take the time to study the problem of a motel room, he can perhaps develop a new type of luggage rack which the buyer will find attractive, and, having sold him one unique unit, talk him into coordinating the room with the use of the craftsman's cocktail table and wood lamp bases.

Remember that in selling to a contract buyer, you represent a departure from his usual kind of source. If he wants a ceramic ashtray, habit has led him to buy a standard glass or white porcelain tray with a decal on it. The idea of a piece distinctive in its appeal and design may well be new to him. Having persuaded him to try one item, your next idea for him will be more easily sold.

One of the nicest things about the contract market is that you can easily reach it and sell it yourself. You can approach the local proprietors or purchasing agents of hotels, motels, better restaurants and chains of establishments. Local architects and decorators usually coordinate the furnishings for new establishments and will be glad to know of your facilities and interest. Your creativity can help them to deliver a more distinctive job. Often, local real estate people will know if a new building is going up and can give you a lead to those persons who are designing or furnishing units in your area.

If you are working in or near a large metropolitan center, the local institutional supply and restaurant supply houses may be a market for you and may even be able to sell your products if you can leave them some samples. The incorporation of emblematic designs in your product can often attract orders from school co-op stores, universities, clubs, and fraternities, as well as from large businesses who want to show their corporate trademarks. Sales, in this market, usually take more time to make but orders can be substantial and profits good.

Products made for institutional use must generally meet more severe utility tests than those you might make for sale to consumers. Briefly, they must meet the common sense criteria of being practical to use and maintain, and they should be sturdy enough in construction and finish to withstand the hard wear characteristic of institutional use and handling methods. They should be difficult for the clientele to put in their pockets unless their adoption is intended. Price is a matter of the buyer and must be seen from his point of view. A college freshman is likely to pay $2.50 for a beer mug with a college seal on it, but he is unlikely to spend $10. An ashtray that a nightclub's customers might take as a souvenir would be expensive at $1, while a yard of handwoven fabric for an important seating piece in a lobby might be acceptable at $40 per yard if esthetically effective.

If you can convince the institutional buyer that the purchase of quality will cost him less in the long run, or if you can show him how a distinctive product will make money for him, he can be sold. Especially on new, large contract jobs, you should be aware of the fact that developing a sale may require a great deal of patience. A lot of planning goes into a new motel, for example, and planning takes time. However, you're not necessarily making a one-time sale. The supervising architect or interior designer may well have another job next week or next month in which your things can be used, and if your articles will break or wear out once in use, there's a good possibility of repeat business.

The proven premise that an institutional market exists for the craftsman is based on the institution's quest for identification and individuality. You must deftly exploit these desires in selling and design and produce to fulfill them. While it is not a prime market for the craftsman to depend upon for day-to-day production demand, the contract market can prove a profitable "plus" for the producing craftsman.

Finally, many contract jobs are prestigious and will be publicized. Don't hesitate to ask the head contractor to include your name and photos of your work in publicity material.

Before going out to sell a contract job, this check list given me by a top purchasing agent who has dealt with craftsmen might well be reviewed. His instructions are: (1) become as familiar as possible with the establishment before making contact; (2) stay close to home. A local craft will be more interesting in a local establishment; (3) see what the establishment needs, and then go back and produce a sample; (4) price the item carefully and determine how many can be supplied and how they can be delivered; (5) then see the purchasing executive.

## THE EXECUTIVE GIFT MARKET

A market closely related to the contract market is the market for business gifts. Frequently, a firm will wish to give its customers a gift which will remind them of the company. This may be done by choosing something so distinctive that it will be a conversation piece (it shouldn't, however, be so distinctive that most people will not want to use or display it!). A firm may not want to use a printed legend, but perhaps an abstraction of its trade insignia.

Some years ago I received a pair of cuff links from a manufacturer of cast aluminum chairs. The design in silver was an attractive simulation of his cast aluminum trade mark. They were an attractive and effective reminder.

Offering a product to the industrial gift buyer requires some research on your part. First, in choosing a company to solicit, be aware that the type of company that sells to others is a better prospect than that which does not. Most gifts are bought for customers. For example, a factory which bought a lot of electronic equipment components to make sub assemblies for one major TV receiver manufacturer would be unlikely to buy many business gifts, whereas the TV manufacturer who sells to major buyers throughout the country might use hundreds of specialized gifts. After determining that an industrial gift buyer buys enough to be a worthwhile client, the next question is how many gifts does he buy according to price range. The Internal Revenue Service will only allow a company to deduct gifts under $25 per person, so that the very large gifts over that amount, not being allowable as a business expense, will be rare.

A firm may buy five $20 gifts, 20 $15 gifts, and 200 $10 gifts. You must know your price before you can begin to think about the items to present.

While you might use an executive gift sales organization, you will probably restrict your sales activity to what you can sell locally. Your costs of sales will be only your own time and travel. Without the markup of middlemen you can earn the retail price for yourself.

A couple of other expenses should be considered as well. Most firms will want their gifts individually packed in an attractive reshipper carton and will expect you to include such packing costs in your price. Furthermore, many will want the manufacturer to label and drop ship the gifts, perhaps sorting and enclosing cards for individual customers. While this is generally covered by a service charge over product cost, be certain it is understood in your purchase agreement with the buyer. You should figure a normal profit on such service activities, just as you do on the cost of manufacture.

When you start to make a business gift, try to build next year's gift into this year's purchase. For example, if a company should purchase a salt and pepper set, you might be able to develop a condiment server in the same price range for the following year, a serving dish the year after, etc. Such product continuity can build sales receptiveness for future years.

Firms differ in their philosophy about business gifts and their ideas of who should actually use them. Some will send an executive a gift picked for use in his home, something his wife will use more often than he. They feel that a gift is a "thank you" for past business. Other firms want something that the buyer himself will use, and most buyers in business are men. Such items will be masculine in appeal and would normally include some original ideas which a man would use in his office, perhaps even on his desk. Such items can include pedestrian ashtrays, or an imaginative desk "caddy." Personal gifts for the man himself are also in order, such as the cuff links mentioned above with a matching tie clip or belt buckle in years to come. Before you start talking product ideation and possibilities with a prospective customer, find out how they feel about the gifts they give.

The executive gift market is almost exclusively a Christmas market. The active selling season seldom begins before late August and all gifts *must* be delivered by December 10th at the latest. Actually, most distributors in this field stated that business started to develop importantly only in mid-to-late September and delivery dates were often set at late November on these same orders. Thus, if you are to follow the same pattern, you would have very little time to make and ship your merchandise. While the professionals in the field book about 70% of their annual business in October and November, there is no reason for you not to solicit business as early as mid-summer. This might help you to turn the mid-summer doldrums into productive selling and manufacturing time. Many commercial firms try for this early business by offering discounts to purchasers for early order placements. Unlike the retail giftware field, executive gift selling requires only a very short line. After all, you will probably be developing a special item for your customers. Even commercial firms in this field might offer only a couple of groups of four or five items each, so tooling is minimized.

If you feel you cannot approach industrial gifts buyers yourself, there are many firms who sell specifically to this trade. The national association of this trade, to which most substantial jobbers and distributors belong, is the Advertising Specialty National Association, 1145 19th Street, N. W., Washington 6, D.C. They can give you information on shows, publications and other channels of contact with this trade. You will note that it is called the "Advertising Specialty" Association. Executive gifts form a small part of the advertising specialty trade. This trade is comprised, in large measure, of people selling low priced junk. They would have little appreciation of a quality craft product and few of the salesmen are geared to selling quality. In general, it's a business that deals in hundreds of thousands of penny items. There are exceptions, of course, and a few dealers and jobbers both appreciate quality and can sell it. They will differ with each area, and you will have to seek them out through the association and its shows.

From a financial point of view there is little advantage in dealing with such a distributor, and several disadvantages. First, he does not buy until he has sold. That means that you carry the risk of inventory and that sales are uncertain. Furthermore, he will hold you to a tight delivery schedule, and there is ample precedent in this field for the event of a salesman suing for his lost commissions or profits if a manufacturer does not meet delivery dates.

Discounts, which amount to sales commissions for the agent, vary widely and are inordinately high. 30% to 50% from list (the price the ultimate industrial buyer pays) are usual, with quality items tending toward 50%. Progressively lower commissions for quantity sales are common, with part of the discount being passed on to the ultimate purchaser.

If you plan to use agents, a catalog becomes a necessity and most catalogs are published in color for this field. This can be expensive. The printing alone of such a color page can cost $200 for the 5,000 you would probably need, and there are many plus costs in preparing a catalog.

For these and many other reasons, it is advisable for the craftsman to work personally in his own area and do his own selling. The executive gift market can be a good supplementary market, but it is not recommended to the craftsman as a prime method of distribution.

## FUND RAISING GROUPS

Few businesses ever think of using fund raising groups as sales organizations. A very few firms do specialize in providing such groups with merchandise to sell as a means of making money, but very few. The few who do, in my experience, have most unimaginative, commonplace things to sell: Christmas cards, or candy. Chances are that there are a number of well organized non-profit groups in your community which constantly need money to carry on their work: fraternal orders, churches, groups to serve disadvantaged youngsters, foreign aid organizations, and school-aid clubs, to mention a few. Their membership is usually made up of capable men and women in the community, and their leaders are well known for community activity. If they can realize a plus-profit for their treasuries by carrying on a simple organized sales program, they may well be interested in working with you or a group of craftsmen.

The best known program of this kind is perhaps the Girl Scout cookie campaign. It is big business and raises millions of dollars. Your local charitable and special interest organizations would probably be interested if you brought them an idea which could raise a few hundred dollars. If you can organize a group of craftsmen in your area to prepare a sales exhibition, and if you offer a percentage of the gross sales, perhaps 25% to a local charitable group, the chances are good that they will provide the posters, carry on the telephone campaign, place the publicity, and do all of the leg-work necessary to bring in the customers. Similarly, a variation of the home-party plan used extensively by some cosmetic and plastic housewares companies can be adapted to selling crafts. An evening is arranged in the home of a group member interested in a particular organization. You might give a talk or a demonstration of your work, alone or with other local craftsmen. The women will know before they come that the object is to buy and that a percentage of the purchase will go to the charity in which they or their friends are interested.

If you have a local shop of your own, or could arrange a temporary one at your studio for a few days, you can often induce local organizations to bulletin or otherwise notify their membership to visit your outlet during specified days. Those who give you an invitation card or mention their organization would then have a percentage of their purchases returned by you to the sponsoring organization.

Fund raising programs of this type call for special attitudes and policies. First, few can buy goods and perhaps this is one of the rare exceptions justifying a "consignment" sale. You are therefore taking more of a risk and should achieve a larger profit. While you might sell a retailer who assumes the risk of purchase and customer service at 50% from your list prices, a maximum of 33% of gross sales might be considered a generous margin for a group of this kind. If you're skillful, they may feel that they are sponsoring you. Let them. Their only profit is in personal satisfaction. When trying to get volunteer groups to do something, it's well to remember that.

In presenting this idea to a group, keep the following points uppermost in your mind. First, they are probably less interested in what they are selling than they are in making money for their cause. Show them how they can make money without risk and you will gain their cooperation. Second, clearly spell out what your responsibilities are and what the group's responsibilities and activities will be.

Will you set up the exhibition or just supervise their people? Will you pay for printed invitations to the show, or will they? What about breakage? Will you deduct it from their profits? A clear understanding can lead to a happy experience which can grow for all concerned in years to come and become an annual event. Also, they are organizing a social activity for their members. Cooperate to make it pleasant.

You can hardly lose on this type of activity if you are not making up special merchandise. Your retailers will seldom object; fighting a good cause is unpopular. Success with one local group may lead you to similar activities nearby. At the very least, the exposure which such an involvement gives you will bring you the attention of other potential buyers in your area. In selecting the group to work with (which, of course, depends in large measure on who wants to work with *you*), remember that you will become identified with that group. It is unlikely that you can work with more than one group in a community, so try to choose the most productive association at the start.

# 10.

## Publicity and Advertising

Aglance at any consumer publication and a visit to the local big consumer goods outlet will together give anyone a capsule picture of the way the majority of goods are sold today in America. Advertising and publicity are depended upon to create either strong initial interest or actual demand. The retail outlet then stocks the goods to fill that demand or anticipated demand. The distribution channel is filled by the manufacturer in anticipation of his also creating the demand which will empty that channel. Unless the mass marketer can move his goods through the channel, largely through his own corporate efforts, it is unlikely that the channel will continue to accept his goods for long. The stores in which you will be approached by a knowledgeable sales person who actually sells you something are becoming all too few. The craftsman having limited, if any, promotional funds must still depend upon the store and store staff to sell his goods. While better specialty outlets still depend on personal selling, the tools of mass communication on which most American marketing has come to depend can still be extremely useful to the craftsman. While there is no craftsman who can consider a page ad in *Life* or *Look* at $35,000 plus for a single issue, and while even small space advertising in such prestigious books as the *New Yorker* or the *Saturday Review* are still fond dreams for most small producers, the avenues of publicity to these same publications are open to anyone with the imagination to use them.

Most people who have not worked in the field look upon editors as super-beings and regard publicity as some other-worldly technique of getting their names before the public. Actually, the process of gaining publicity is a simple, common sense procedure which you can grasp and use. A working definition of publicity might be the obtaining of free exposure for yourself or your product. Some commonplace examples would include a newspaper article about you or your work or a magazine feature covering your activities or product. A display in a bank window might also be considered publicity, as would a credit line on a published photograph using your merchandise.

To call this exposure free is perhaps something of a misstatement. Certainly the magazine or newspaper space, or bank window is given to you without charge for the space. If you can get yourself on a TV or radio program to show and talk about your work, no charge will be made for air time. The costs of publicity are largely costs of effort, and you must be prepared to invest substantial time and energy and perhaps to purchase photos for publication. You'll be asked to loan samples with the possibility that some may be damaged or lost, and perhaps you'll want to make a gift of one of your things to an editor. You'll have to work to obtain publicity and your work has value. You should be selective in its investment.

In overcoming your initial shyness about selling yourself to obtain publicity, you might well ask yourself why anyone would want to talk about you. To help dispel your inertia, let's take a look at a few of the reasons why the craftsman might be worthy of publicity. First, the job of an editor is to fill the published space, air time, or display areas for which he is responsible with information and material that will interest people. Editors have as much trouble obtaining unusual material as you might feel you would have in placing it. Therefore, they're interested in "leads." As a living, breathing craftsman, you are, in a sense, unique. Our society of anonymous masses looks upon the crafts as glamorous and exciting. Most people would love to possess a strong individual identity; to make beautiful things, to be identified with them and to live independently from their manufacture and sale. Unfortunately, the would-be independents may lack the courage or the talent to make it possible for them to do what you are doing. They identify with something they admire, however, much as the weekend sailor identifies with the adventurous man who crosses the Atlantic in a 13 foot sailboat. For these reasons and others, you may be news.

More exactly, you may be able to make yourself news. Making yourself news locally is going to be a lot easier than getting any kind of national notice. The very fact that you are a part of a local community and doing something different may be enough reason for the local press to give you space.

Perhaps you occupy some well known building in your work, or there may be some historical connection between what you are doing and what was done in your area in the past. Furthermore, the local editor or radio station is not presented with as much material from which to choose stories or program developments as a major communications organization in a big city, and they are likely to welcome your request more readily. If you are marketing locally, such grass roots activity may be the most effective publicity you can have. Something as simple as a display of your products in the lobby of the local resort hotel, should there be one, opens the possibility of bringing buyers to you who are already in your own area. The hotel manager may be more than willing to give you such a display because it will make his guests' stay more interesting. Further, working locally with sympathetic people can give you an insight into the procedures which will later make approaches to more important media of exposure easier.

You must have a central idea or theme before you ask for exposure. In brief, there must be something for your editor to talk about. The fact that you exist is not enough. The idea which you present to an editor should be as exciting and timely as possible. If you are making jewelry, rather than talking about your jewelry alone, you might take the approach of relating your work to current trends in sculpture and painting.

If your craft has historical importance, you ought to present enough research material to show what was done in years past and demonstrate its relationship to what you are doing. Personalities are always good for some exposure, and if the person is well enough known to the audience, an editor will be eager. A visit by the governor's wife to your shop or studio could be a newsworthy event, and especially so if you can get a photo of the lady in the shop with you. Don't hesitate to ask such people to cooperate with you. If they are interested in what you are doing, they will generally be delighted. After all, it gives them exposure too.

If you are a potter, you might consider working with a prominent local garden club to develop a program on flower arranging, using your pots for the arrangement. Invite the local editors and broadcasters to attend. A prize you win in a competition can be reason enough for the release of information, as can your success in selling in other parts of the country. The prominence of a local man is always a source of pride.

If you approach national media, let's say magazines like *American Home* or *Vogue,* the material which you present to them must be of national interest, and specifically, of potential interest to their readers. What will interest their readers is best indicated by what they now print editorially and by the type of product advertising which they carry. For example, if your product is pottery, you might attempt to prepare a release showing how beautiful art objects (which incidentally you produce) can add beauty to everyday living in the forms of cookware, ashtrays, drinking vessels, etc.

The editor might well develop a suggested theme of this kind showing other things in addition to those you make, but if he was excited enough by what you sent to develop your idea (now his) he would almost certainly include your things importantly. Such a subject has national appeal and would be a reasonable editorial approach.

Approaches to publicity are almost limitless, and no list of examples could possibly be long enough. If there existed somewhere a list of publicity ideas, they would all be of questionable value because of the fact that someone had already used them. Ask yourself what you think might be the most interesting aspects of your work to an outsider. If you have friends who are wise enough to be frank with you, ask them. Locally, invite an editor to come by for a visit or a luncheon, and be frank in stating that you think you have a story to tell, but are not quite sure how to go about it. Nobody will laugh at an honest approach that lacks expertise. Listen to the people who buy from you. They may give you ideas for presenting your products by reacting to what you have.

Almost everybody likes publicity, but too few realize what publicity can do for them apart from ego satisfaction. Publicity is a sales tool. Its purpose is to help you to move merchandise. If it doesn't do that, it is of questionable value. If you cannot see, pretty directly, how it will serve that end, it is probably a waste of time. This is not to say that a given article is supposed to create sales for a given product, although it can do that, too. Any exposure which will tend to identify your product, tell a potential customer where it can be bought, or strengthen your image or the image of what you make can result in sales. It can result in sales, if, along with presenting your goods, the publicity also tells the audience what it is and where it can be obtained. Most commercial firms will not lend merchandise to an editor except in exchange for a credit line which does that. Of course, there are times when you'll be called upon by an editor to lend props in a situation where he cannot give your products credit, but then it's the matter of building good will that may lead you to cooperate.

As a merchant, it is important that you understand how to use publicity. Timing publicity is perhaps the most important factor of all, and most beginners are prone to forget this is in their enthusiasm to be publicized. If a piece of publicity is premature, it most often constitutes an opportunity wasted, and it is difficult to regain that lost exposure quickly. An editor can only talk about you at infrequent intervals. Suppose that you, as a consumer, see something in your morning paper that interests you and that you think you might like to own. You have read the article and the natural reaction is to think of when you might go to see the goods. If it is a low priced purchase, in your terms, one that does not require financial planning, you will probably just decide to go and look at it, and if it is still desirable, to buy it. You might be excited by the whole idea of a shop or exhibit and decide that on your next opportunity, you'll go to visit it. If, on the other hand, there is no place you can go at the time you read the article, you'll quickly forget about what you've seen, most likely, and not be attracted to the merchandise or shop until you are next reminded of it by something else.

Thus, a first rule might be not to waste publicity until there is some place where the reader can see and buy your product immediately. Publicity may not actually sell your product for you, but it can support sales by calling attention to your outlet, and with repeated exposure, consumer interest and sales will develop. Another conflict between ego and sales arises in the matter of giving credits. Let us suppose that you are given a free exhibition space at a local fair but that you cannot sell there. A placard will most likely tell the viewer what he is looking at. You have the natural desire to see your name and your story prominently displayed on the product. However, if you are not prepared to handle consumer sales directly, it is much more sensible to credit a dealer to whom you sell. Probably both you and your dealer can be credited in this fashion: hand painted tole available at the Craft Corner, 20 Main Street, Marketown. Designed and produced by Jane Smith of East Craftown. However, all of your publicity should give your sales outlet the first and most important credit. The object is to attract customers.

In addition to bringing customers to you or your outlets, publicity has re-use value. When you've collected some good clippings, these can become a valuable part of your sales kits. Pasted on a board and photostated with the title "head" of the publication in which they appeared, they will lend authority to a presentation. In this respect, they are more valuable than advertising. Anyone with the price can buy an ad, but someone genuinely admired your work before writing an article on it. It thus constitutes an authoritative endorsement of your work. A regular flow of such publicity presentation material can not only be a fine tool for a salesman, but will tend to increase his confidence in what you are doing. Publicity can be believed by everyone except the person publicized!

While slightly more expensive than photostats, a photo offset of your publicity clippings can make an excellent mailing piece. One mailed out to your customers with a new price list, for example, will tend to keep you in the public mind and stimulate interest in your product. A reprint of this kind, with a brief sales message, is a perfectly good excuse for a simple and interesting mail piece. If you have a shop, it can serve as a give-away. The nicest thing about publicity, and, as you will soon learn, its greatest danger, is that in the mind of communications-conscious Americans publicity equals success. The illusion of success is very desirable, even when the facts don't warrant it, because success breeds confidence in the value of your product. But the beneficiary can be overly optimistic. I am personally acquainted with two examples of important publicity in *Life* Magazine which will serve here as illustrations.

One of America's top designers created a line of contemporary birdhouses. They were extremely well made by a highly reputable factory and well priced. *Life* made a magnificent photograph of them, and many stores were sold the units and special displays prepared in anticipation of their appearance in *Life*. Sales to consumers were scarce and few reorders developed. The line was withdrawn from the market several months later, never to be seen again. The publicity failed to produce significant sales. In

*Life,* at roughly the same time, skiers were shown on the cover wearing whimsical ski masks from Peru. Customers wrote to the importer by the thousands and tens of thousands of dollars were reportedly made from this single exposure which successfully introduced a new product to the market. It should be noted, in the case of the birdhouses that failed, that the distributors of the product took advantage of the forthcoming publicity as a tool to make dealers purchase and importantly display the products. It could well have been the case that, while the publicity failed to pull responses in terms of developing purchases, the product, well displayed in many stores as a result of the anticipated publicity, could have succeeded on its own. You cannot always know in advance when publicity will break, but when you do it should be used actively and intensively as a sales tool to place merchandise.

If all salesmen are designers, then all editors would like to behave like merchandisers. Ideally, publicity should be used to support sales of your best items. It is sometimes necessary to offer an editor a "shocker," a far out design which makes good copy but which doesn't sell. In such cases, that kind of exposure is better than none and you will go along with what the editor likes; but, if possible, get some of your staple articles into the showing. If you are so fortunate as to be able yourself to select the articles to be featured, suppress your esthetic instincts if they don't coincide with commercial results, and show the items that sell. A show piece is a luxury which can and should be included if space permits, but not if a choice must be made.

Just as a fine product in the wrong store will fail to sell, the right publicity reaching the wrong audience or breaking at a bad time will be a wasted effort. Try to match the media to your product. A couple of oversimplified examples will serve to make the point. You have some charming embroidered aprons. The Public Relations office of a local brewery approaches you to make a special one for use in his TV commercial. On checking, you find that he sponsors the telecasts of the local wrestling matches and is doing barbecue type commercials to appeal to men. The chances of your apron making a significant impression, even if importantly reviewed, are close to nil. Don't use it. If the local food editor wants to show a kitchen picture in her daily cooking column and will use an apron you have, it's probably an opportunity—worth the small effort, but marginal. The woman reading the receipe of the day is food-conscious, not dress-conscious, but at least you're being exposed to women. If, on the other hand, you're supplying some samples to the local women's page editor who is doing a column on dressing for home entertaining and serving, you have found the right context, and placing your apron with her makes your effort worthwhile.

We are back to the subject of whom to contact and how. You've decided, tentatively at least, that editors are approachable. You have an idea concerning your work which you think is interesting enough to propose. You have chosen the medium you think best for presenting your story. Finally, you've examined your idea and its presentation and have satisfied yourself that it will help you to sell your wares. Whom do you contact?

A local newspaper, with a phone call, will tell you who edits the section in which you are interesed. Similarly, the name of the person responsible for producing a local TV or radio show can be obtained by calling the station. A direct statement of the nature of your interest should lead you to the person who will be handling your material. Out of town newspapers are more of a problem. A book called *Working Press of the Nation* is the best guide and may be available from your library. It lists publications and their editors in all fields with their departmental responsibilities. *Working Press of the Nation* is published by the National Research Bureau, Inc., 221 North LaSalle Street, Chicago, Illinois. Volumes covering Newspaper, Magazine, and Radio and TV editors are released annually at a cost of $30 each. Often school or public libraries have copies for reference.

Magazines usually publish their own editor listings in every issue by way of giving the editors who produce the magazine credit for their work. This section is called the "mast head" and generally appears in the first few pages of a publication. If you're not entirely sure which editor is right, make a guess. Your communication will generally be passed along to the correct person, even if you make an error.

Most people prefer to see and talk to the person they're dealing with. If you can arrange to call and meet the editor you're interested in, you'll learn more about him than if you must communicate by mail. However, communicating by mail will serve as an introduction and is preferable to no contact at all. You must remember that you cannot make demands in obtaining publicity. Even after you have submitted your copy, photos, or samples, you can have no assurance of what will appear or when it will appear. In fact, it may even be outside the editor's control. Putting together a publication is a complicated job. Decisions have to be made by the magazine which will produce the best book or paper at a given moment. Advertisers are assured of getting what they wanted but of course they paid for it. As a person seeking publicity, you did not buy your exposure. If you are disappointed, the only thing you can do is say "thanks" to the people you have been working with and try again in the near future. Persistence can pay. At some point you will deliver what an editor can use. If he feels your things are of no interest to him, he'll politely let you know.

The basic written form for presenting your material to an editor is the "press release." For routine news information the press release may be reproduced by a publication as is, in whole, or in part. If a feature story is in prospect, editors will want more information and will be in personal touch with you. Although TV and radio people do not present their information from a printed form, the standard press release can also serve them as introductory information.

A press release is a conventional format for releasing news to those who may republish it. While it has certain characteristics, the approach to writing releases will vary as greatly as the number of creative people producing them. A few of the definable characteristics are common to most news releases:

1. The release states by whom it is released at the top of the first page.
2. It shows a release date on which or after which the editor may print the information it contains. You may say for "immediate release," or you may wish to release it at some near future time to coordinate with a store promotional showing. (In that case you would put the date of the store opening.)

A press release should be brief. It should present the idea just as you would like to see it reproduced in a publication. Because space is valuable, your news release will probably be altered or cut and you should write your release in a "V" shape.

That is, you should place the most intriguing and important information at the top of the release. Less important and less vital information should follow with the least vital facts and developments last. Thus, if a publication cuts your copy, the more important facts will still be there because cutting is generally done at the bottom.

It is general practice to add a line to a release stating "for further information contact:" followed by the name, address and phone number of the person to be called. If the release is of interest you will be called. You do not have to force every last fact into the release. An effort to do so will probably obscure your basic and central thought.

A word must be said about exclusivity in releasing material. Two or more publications may be competitive. For example, if your city has two morning papers, they would be competitive. If you wish to send them both information, you should make the fact known that the release date is to be observed. When photographs are included, they should be different for each competitive paper. In the case of magazines, because they work so much further in advance and generally deal in features rather than news, the same material should not be simultaneously submitted to two competing publications, i.e. *Life,* and *Look* or *House and Garden* and *House Beautiful.* Exclusivity is expected even if not asked for, and should be granted. Failure to observe this rule in publicity can make you many enemies more quickly than any other mistake.

SCHERR & McDERMOTT INTERNATIONAL in cooperation with the ALLIANCE FOR PROGRESS and with the AGENCY FOR INTERNATIONAL DEVELOPMENT

☐REPLY TO MADISON AVENUE OFFICE ☐REPLY TO FIFTH AVENUE OFFICE

INTRODUCING

## PRODUCTS OF THE ALIANZA

A new approach to self-help in Latin America has been developed with the cooperation of the Alliance for Progress and four co-founding countries - Columbia, Ecuador, Peru, and Bolivia.

A Marketing and Product Development Center operating under the name of PRODUCTS OF THE ALIANZA has been established at 7610 Empire State Building, New York City, for the purpose of marketing a variety of the handicraft and light industry products from the four participating Latin American countries. The sales activities will be geared to North American merchants and distributors, as well as the European market. The Center is working with importing distributors, designers, manufacturers who require special materials or component parts, and larger retailers capable of importation. The Center provides assistance in design, purchasing, product development, sampling, and order control service - at no charge - to the interested individuals or groups.

This program was promulgated in 1961 and has been recently reaffirmed by President Johnson. It is being conducted on a non-profit basis by the Cooperative League of the USA under contract with AID. Headquarters are in Washington, D.C., and Mr. Donald E. Kramer is Project Manager.

Suite 707, 79 Madison Avenue/New York, New York 10016, U.S.A. Telephone (212) 889-4280 Cable NYESMAK NEWYORK
Showroom: Suite 329, 225 Fifth Avenue/New York, New York 10010, U.S.A. Telephone (212) 889-4280

To give you an idea of what a professional press release looks like, one is reproduced on page 104. Even a typed page following this general format will readily be recognized for what it is.

Releases should be accompanied by some good photos. It goes without saying that they should illustrate as clearly as possible what your release tells in words. They will be well received if they are 8 x 10 glossy prints, as that is the print which publications are used to working with. If you are fortunate enough to excite interest in color reproductions, the publication will usually wish to send its own photographer to make the pictures, or will request that you ship merchandise to them to be photographed at their expense.

At the start of this chapter advertising was given second place for the craftsman. This is not because advertising is less useful than publicity, but rather because the cost of effective advertising is generally beyond the reach of most small craftsmen and not warranted to support the sale of limited production. However, there are several ways in which you can consider using advertising when your growth permits, and these must be noted.

Your qualification is a matter of volume. While it will vary, an annual volume of at least $50,000 wholesale is perhaps a break point at which you can consider advertising. A high advertising budget might be considered 5% of your total volume, and, with a few exceptions, $2,500 per year could be considered a workable minimum budget. The few exceptions where a small budget might be productive would include advertising such as the following:

Striking, repetitive classified ads in a local paper; in a resort area the publications placed in guest rooms generally afford an inexpensive means of reaching visitors; a sign or a billboard on the highway going through your area. Other such inexpensive devices may be well worth your consideration. Advertising costs generally vary directly with the number of people the medium can reach. If you are wholesaling your product, chances are that the trade publication which goes to the small but highly select group of dealers is a valid investment. In most circumstances this will be a wiser investment than the same money spent on a consumer publication. When you get to the point of preparing actual advertising, you must remember that there are more costs involved than the cost of space alone. Someone must design your ad, set type, and probably have a good photo made. All these elements must then be turned into a paste-up or mechanical which is an exact original of the advertisement. Unless photo offset is used, you'll have the cost of a plate to pay. All of these preparations require professional skill, and it would be well to seek out the services of a graphic artist who is used to working with publications or an advertising agency which will handle the whole job for you.

Advertising on a limited budget has always raised the question of whether one large ad is preferable to a number of small ones. My preference has always been multiple exposure in small spaces rather than one or two full page ads.

The size of the minimum acceptable space depends on the nature of the publication, and you should review the ads in several issues of the book you intend to use before placing your ads. Good design will often make a small ad as striking and effective as a large one.

The timing of an ad is similarly important, and you must husband your budget to excite buying during peak periods. For example, if your prime retail market period in your own store is November and December, your ads should appear in October and November. If your principal markets come in January and June, your ads should appear in pre-market trade publications.

An advertising agency can be of great help to you. In fact, for any substantial advertising program a good agency is almost essential. They can help you to decide how to use your budget most wisely by selecting the right media to your best advantage. Since an ad agency's stock in trade is creative service, and since they can only make money selling that service, their thinking will cost you money. You will have to be the judge of the quality of the service you are buying. A small agency can be good, particularly for a small budget. A poor agency can result in the loss of the money you have put aside for advertising.

Agencies make money in three ways. They receive a commission on space which is paid to them by the publications in which they place advertising. It is normally 15% of the billed space cost. If you were going to buy $5,000 worth of space in publications during the year, your agency could expect to make only $750.

Since they can afford to do only a limited amount of work for $750, they may also have to charge you for their creative services. These include the work of their copywriters, art directors, and the art staff people who will prepare your mechanicals and put an ad together. Their production people will handle the purchasing of the plates, and, if required, photography. All this is time and overhead and must be charged to the client. If your budget is small, an agency that finds itself spending more time than your purchase of space and services will pay for may also charge a monthly retainer fee. All these costs are legitimate if the agency produces work good enough to justify them, but they may make an advertising program impossible for you.

Based on your volume, you will set aside a percentage for advertising, and this will become your budget. As your business increases, so should your budget. The first question to be answered is whether or not your budget is adequate to do an effective job. One ad may be good for your ego, but it is questionable that a single insertion can develop business.

Generally speaking, unless you can enter a monthly publication at least three times a year, you had better forget any ad plans until you have grown.

Your budget must be your agency's budget. If a few agencies are interviewed and most of them honestly tell you that you cannot make an effective presentation for your budget, be skeptical of the exception that tells you they can perform within the budget.

In order to meet overhead and make a normal profit an agency must charge you two to three times their cost of labor, and creative advertising people are expensive. Be cautious if they are promising you more than you can pay for. While occassionally an agency will trim its fees somewhat for an opportunity to do a creative "prestige" ad or to get an account they feel will grow, they will not lose money on an account for long.

One of the most sensible ways to be economical in advertising is to make one good ad and use it again and again. While the space must be paid for each time, the preparatory work and the plate can be reused. The cost of make-ready can often exceed the cost of space in low cost trade media, for example, and an "institutional" ad which relies on projecting an image rather than selling a specific group of merchandise can be used repeatedly and is a sensible approach to advertising on a limited budget.

If you have decided that you can afford and need advertising beyond the local level, and you must choose an agency, you should shop for one just as you do for anything else that you buy. It is important that the people who will be responsible for producing your advertising understand the feeling of your product and you can accept your image. Don't hesitate to ask to talk with the art director and the copy chief. Employ the agency where your ideas seem to be comfortably accepted. When you have made your choice of an agency, don't hesitate to participate in the creation of the ad. I have heard account men tell clients, "You produce the merchandise, we'll produce the ad." In part this is true. They know or should know better than you how best to construct an ad to motivate the reader.

However, you are the one who knows what you want that ad to do, and you must work closely with the creative people in order to explain to them what you are trying to say and the "look" you want to achieve.

There are all types of agencies. Small ones are often little more than graphic arts services, and perhaps this is all a small advertiser will need. Agencies can perform a variety of other services which you will surely need as you grow. These include the preparation of catalogs (although you can often accomplish this by working directly with a creative printer), tags and labels, point of sale display devices, direct mail pieces, etc. These secondary services may be reason enough for establishing a relationship with an ad agency if the talents required to produce these sales tools are not otherwise available to you.

In closing this chapter it seems necessary to restate the warning of its opening thoughts. While Americans tend to regard advertising as magical, it is not. It is basically a mass communications technique for solving mass marketing problems. A little bit of advertising, like a little bit of medicine, can be worthless. Publicity is a useful sales tool which almost anyone can afford if willing to invest the time which it requires.

# 11.

# Some Legal Pointers
# for the Craftsman in Business

If you were to ask a dozen designers or creative people around New York who the "creating-man's lawyer" is, the name of attorney Lee Epstein would probably come up six times. A man with a formidable legal background, Mr. Epstein has long been associated with the creative professions as an educator. The legal opinions expressed in this chapter are mainly counselor Epstein's, and they reflect his view that the purpose of attention to the legal aspects of business is to prevent litigation.

The first legally oriented problem you will face as a craftsman in business is the legal structure of your business. As the sole owner of a business which makes and sells merchandise, you are, or will be, operating as a single proprietorship. If your business operates under your name and nothing more, you need not take any step other than opening your door to trade. If, however, you add so much as the words "Studio" or "Associates" to your name, you must register your business name. This is done, very simply, at your county clerk's office for a nominal fee, $50 in New York State. On registering your business name, if you obtain an extra copy of your registration for another $1 or so, it can be given to your bank to open a business account.

Under a single proprietorship, the simplest form of business organization, the owner's business and private affairs are treated as one for the purpose of dealing with creditors.

Note, then, that personal assets such as your car, home, stocks, savings, etc., can be reached by your creditors to cover a liability incurred by the business. Thus, an accident or claim arising from any business circumstance can make you personally liable.

A partnership occurs when two or more persons combine for the purpose of doing business. Such business can be carried on under a trade name or under the names of the partners. Either must be registered with the county clerk. This is often called a "joint venture." Though the partnership agreement may not divide profits equally among the partners, all partners are equally liable for any debts. If one partner cannot pay his share of a claim against the business, the total fortunes of all other partners are available to satisfy the total demands of any creditor of the partnership. Despite their joint responsibilities, partners are taxed as individuals.

For all but the small or very new business, and perhaps even then, the most advantageous form of organization today is almost always the corporation. A corporation is an entity created under a state statute which lays down certain requirements. These concern the number of stockholders needed to found a corporation (though later ownership may be concentrated in one person), the number and powers of directors, the calling of stockholders' meetings, audits, etc. Forming a corporation is a simple matter and should not frighten the new businessman.

A corporation operates as though it were a person. Stockholders are liable only to the extent of their contribution to the business, except in extraordinary circumstances. A corporation is immortal and, in the absence of an agreement to the contrary, does not cease to exist on the death of a stockholder. The advantages of a corporation are many and should be discussed with your accountant, from the standpoint of taxes, as well as with an attorney. In addition to the principals' liability being limited to the amount of their investment, the assets of the company are also beyond reach of an individual's creditors. For example, let's suppose that you as an individual or one of your partners acquires a private liability arising out of an automobile accident. As a private entrepreneur, the assets of your business are in jeopardy. If it is your partner's accident, his creditors can reach his share of the partnership, if necessary forcing liquidation of the business. A potter might make a teapot which one day, when filled with boiling water, drops while being handled and scalds someone. As the maker of the product, you are liable if the injured party can prove your product was inherently dangerous or defective. If a visitor to your store or workshop should have an accident, you may again find yourself in trouble. Regardless of the form of business organization you establish, the possibilities of incurring a liability are many and the corporate structure tends to protect you.

Before you start your business, you should definitely make arrangements with a reputable local insurance agent to cover these and other obvious risks. Owner-landlord-tenant policies, workman's compensation, product liability insurance, and other forms of protection may well be indicated in your situation and will give you peace of mind as well as protection.

As your business grows and becomes profitable, the fact that significant tax savings are possible to a corporation will become important to you. Pension and profit-sharing plans offer legitimate tax shelters in the years of greatest earnings under a corporate structure. Briefly, a pension plan or profit-sharing arrangement permits a participant to put away tax free a substantial part of his earnings and to accumulate income on that part without paying taxes on it as earned income. If withdrawn later, these are taxable, but generally at a lower rate than during your peak earning years.

Other more familiar tax advantages may also arise out of a corporate structure. If you deduct a car for business use, you are not likely to be questioned on it if a corporation owns the car and claims its cost as a business expense. This is true of many business expenses which are paid directly by the corporation and not by way of reimbursement to the employees. Lee Epstein points out, "the more prosperous a corporation is, the greater the allowance for expenses; while the more prosperous an individual is, the more closely his return is examined."

Whether or not you even think about it, your business will have a legal form, if only as a sole proprietorship. Some thought should be given at the outset to the form that will serve you best.

The ownership of a business may change as time passes. A partnership exists only so long as the partners remain the same, whereas stock in a corporation, representing ownership, can easily be transferred from one person to another without any outward change in the company as far as your customers are concerned.

Once your business legally exists, the next legal question that troubles most creative people and designers in business is that of protecting their designs. From a businessman's point of view, most concern that is given to the protection of designs is important as a matter of attitude rather than an important financial consideration. Before proceeding to Mr. Epstein's published opinion on design protection, with which you should indeed be familiar, it would be well to put the importance of the matter in proper working perspective.

As a craftsman, you are or should be working well ahead of market trends. If a manufacturer is to be tempted to copy your designs, he must be convinced of a number of things: (1) that a particular item is selling well (I have seen many of the "knock-off artists" copy the wrong item, or copy something long after it had reached its sales peak); (2) that he can make a high, or higher than normal profit on the item he is about to copy; (3) that he can sell it in volume sufficient to support economical production at his level; (4) that you have not protected your design, or at least will not fight a copy legally. The first consideration is very difficult to define for the would-be copier. He perhaps sees an article in a retail store and is advised by the sales person that it is moving well. As we all know, an item that does well in one store will not necessarily do well in another. Therefore, the information he receives may be misinformation. If he habitually copies, he may be aware of this risk. On the other hand, he may have observed the item for a significant period of time before deciding to simulate it. In this case the item is already an established style, and unless you have created a classic that cannot be significantly improved upon, he will probably do you little harm with his copy. It has been my experience that the copier more frequently than not either copies a poor item or copies an item too late. The same lack of creativity which leads him to copy also indicates a lack of judgment as to what he will copy.

Next, he faces the problem of "copying down" your item. He must make an attractive profit, or think that he will, or there is no point in his running the risk of copying. To reach a greater market, he will most often try to reduce price, and to do this he must change the item in quality and character. Even if the change is little more than a change in finish or material, it ceases to be the original which presumably you have crafted with some integrity.

The responsible craftsman is producing merchandise that is valued for its integrity of manufacture as well as for its imaginative design. The copy is most often obviously different.

If you price one of your best items too high, you will be inviting its reproduction. An experienced producer can estimate the cost of producing an item that falls into his type of production, and, if he sees an excessive profit, will be tempted by it. It is wise, therefore, when you find that an item is widely marketable, to re-examine your pricing structure and hold yourself to a normal profit. The exception to this, of course, is a situation in which you believe you have found some short-cut to make an item which you do not believe can be easily duplicated. In such cases your higher profit can simply be considered a plus-reward for your manufacturing ingenuity.

As a craftsman, another manufacturer will look upon you as a limited producer, and will perhaps be tempted to copy your work by the prospect of servicing a broader market. There are dangers present for the person who is going to reproduce your design, but this won't help you. To adapt your product for what the producer thinks is a broader market, he will almost invariably "improve" the product, thereby destroying its inherent character. Furthermore, the article which proves salable in limited "class" markets will frequently fail to succeed in mass outlets.

Some years ago, one of the major clock manufacturers produced a line very reminiscent of a group marketed by a small clock manufacturer. The major company failed to achieve the broad market expected and found the line unprofitable in limited production. The promotion which they did ultimately helped the smaller manufacturer to broaden his market by creating a broader demand for his type of product. If you are creating products suitable to your market and keeping your quality and esthetic standards high, the risk of losing your market to another firm will be substantially reduced.

Finally, while practical protection can be achieved within limits, it is only as good as your willingness to institute legal action to enjoin another maker from using your designs. This judgment should be a matter of business and not of emotion. You must ask yourself if the cost of protecting a design through legal action is warranted by the potential profits which will accrue to you in keeping the market to yourself. Most often, in the craft fields, it will not.

Once you have decided that a design is worth protecting there are various methods of protecting it. We have already noted that if the craftsman is working in a truly creative and exciting way, he will inspire others to produce work not unlike his own. When the design you produce merely suggests a direction to another designer or producer, and he produces similar items, be flattered. You cannot claim remuneration as a source of inspiration. On the other hand, if a direct copy is made, you can claim protection and possibly payment for the use of your design.

If your work can be classified as a work of art, the simplest, cheapest, and most effective way to protect it is by means of a copyright. Copyrights apply only to works of art, but the changing of a work of art into a useful object does not invalidate the copyright protection. For example, if you copyright a piece of ceramic sculpture, the fact that a company drills and mounts it as a lamp would not change its protected status. To copyright a work of art, you simply send two photographs of the object with a completed blank supplied free by the Copyright Office and a four dollar fee to: Register of Copyright, Library of Congress, Washington, D.C. In due course, the copy of the application will be returned to you, stamped by the Copyright Office to indicate the date on which it was filed. The Copyright Office makes no attempt to determine whether or not the design originated with you, and an infringer may seek to defeat your claim to originality by showing that the design is not, in fact, originally yours. Such a copyright is good for 28 years and may be renewed for another 28 years. As a practical matter, the fact that you have filed a copyright may dissuade an infringer from continuing to make your design if he knows you have moved to protect it and has been advised that you intend to take legal action. He, too, must decide whether the cost of defending his action legally is worthwhile, not only in terms of potential profits he hopes to make, but also in terms of his reputation in a style field. The threat of action on your part may be sufficient either to stop production or to lead the firm that copied to a mutually acceptable royalty arrangement with you.

Unlike copyright protections, in order to obtain a patent, the object in question must exhibit some form of originality or invention. If your design is a useful object, and therefore not subject to copyright protection, you can protect it by a design patent which protects its mode of operation.

Patent laws are designed to multiply inventions and to bring them into use, but they are also intended to prevent monopolies from falling into the hands of people who have not actually created something new. Therefore, when an applicant files to obtain a patent, the Patent Office will make a thorough search of its files to make certain that nothing like it has been patented before. The patent examiner will try to prove, through an investigation of the literature in the field, from museum collections and any other available sources, that in fact the invention is not new. Only if he cannot prove "prior art," that is to say, the prior existence of idea, will you be given a patent.

In writing for the American Craftsmen's Council in 1964, Lee Epstein states, "Design patents are a kind of hybrid but are affected by the fact that they are issued by the Patent Office.

"All that a design patent protects is the appearance of an object. This does not mean, as some people believe, that infringement can be avoided by making a minute change in the appearance of a patented object. The real test is whether an unwary observer, seeing the two objects separately (not side by side, so that the differences are emphasized) will think that they are identical or substantially identical." Mr. Epstein goes on to point out that design patents cost perhaps $150-200 each, as contrasted with a $4 copyright fee, and perhaps more if unusual complications arise in the filing of the patent. In obtaining a design patent the originator would be well advised to employ the services of an attorney competent in this field and not attempt to carry on the patent procedure himself.

While you may think that a design patent gives you greater protection, it is a fact that the courts have actually invalidated patents more often than copyrights. You, as the holder of a design patent, would have to bear the burden of proving that your design is unlike any other design. In conclusion Lee Epstein suggests that the copyright is the sounder of the two means of protection and that, "After all, an artist doesn't create his art out of whole cloth; he sees something that the crowd sees, but he sees it in a different light, from a different point of view, with a different eye." Your contribution is more likely to be artistic innovation or originality than actual invention. Therefore, in many instances, the judicious use of the copyright can give you some protection with a minimum of cost and difficulty.

Perhaps following some rules of the work-a-day world in regard to design protection can be more useful to you than a preoccupation, at every turn, with your legal rights. The best protection you can give yourself is not to expose a really new idea which you think will create a market demand until you are ready to service that demand. If your outlets have customers wanting more than you can make of an object, they are likely to talk about it and encourage someone else to leap in to fill their needs. If you see, from early exposure, that you have an idea which is truly a mass market idea giving rise to a demand you are incapable of filling, you should take the initiative. Your experience in sales of the item could well lead a reputable manufacturer to make the object in quantity and pay you a royalty for the use of your design. By seeking out a manufacturer and inducing him to put it into production, you will receive credit for your work, royalty income, and usually keep some control over the quality and final appearance of the item produced. There is no better sales "pitch" for your designs than your own proven sales.

Of all means of design protection, perhaps the best weapon is your skill as an innovator. If you or your salesman find that one of your accounts will buy your products and, when a "knock-off" comes along, will give his business to the firm copying your designs, you should make it clear that he will be the loser. He will be trading the sales potential of one copy for a future in which he can continue to present your innovations first in his market.

If his shop the right kind of outlet for you, he should quickly see that your line, being first consistently, will be worth more to him than a fast profit on a few copied items.

If you honestly believe that you are truly creative and gain satisfaction from working creatively, you should not be worried about the copy or two that may develop in the course of your working career. If you are constantly moving ahead in your design thinking, your reputation will be built on that fact rather than on a given design or two.

Other legal problems are much more likely to become practical matters for you in business than design protection. They are talked about less than design ownership because they are less likely to be emotional involvements.

As you develop catalogs, publicity material, and exhibits, you will be taking pictures. Many of these will show people. A large educational toy company was recently sued by one of its former designers for the use of his children's pictures in its annual catalog. When the designer brought his children in to be photographed, he was fully aware of the purpose to which the pictures would be put, and he and his employer were on friendly terms. After he left the company, he filed suit. Although he lost, the company's cost of defending the suit was substantial. Note that if photos are used by you for any commercial purpose, you should have a legal photo release signed by the person photographed. Such releases are sold by large photographic dealers and your local photo dealer can undoubtedly obtain a pad of printed releases for you for a dollar or two.

If not, he can surely tell you where to buy them. If you are embarrassed about asking your friends or employees to sign them, just explain that your printer or perhaps your ad agency requires them. If someone won't sign a release, don't use the photograph.

Your relationship with your salesman may also have legal implications for your business. If your salesman is an independent contractor, you probably do not have to bother with workman's compensation insurance for him, but if you control the details and amount of his performance, he's legally an employe no matter how you may pay him. Persons working in your studio or factory, of course, are so controlled and should definitely be covered by compensation insurance.

Claims against you can similarly arise from the fact that when you sell a product, you often give a warrantee whether or not you express it. Certain warrantees are implied by law and are inherent in the maker-seller posture you assume as a producing craftsman. Most of these are covered by the attitude of the good businessman who stands behind his product, and they need not be matters of great concern. However, when you sell, you do warrant merchandisability. This means that the goods are not defective or "seconds" and that their quality is such that they can be resold. In practice, your goods should be as good or better than your sample.

When you accept a special commission another kind of problem may arise from the fact that you may be prescribing for a special situation. For example, if you are sculpting in metal and a customer asks you to do a piece to place in a fountain, it is implied that the piece will not rust and disintegrate. If it does, your customer may not only be able to claim the cost of the sculpture, but also damages to his pool as well. Fabrics woven to color match will surely not be a perfect match to other textiles in the room and will in time fade. Therefore, you must specify a "reasonable" match and offer no guarantee of color fastness beyond that given you by the maker of the yarns you employ, or better than that, no guarantee at all.

Whether or not you specifically empower him to do so, your salesman can also commit you. He has, by the nature of his position with you, the implied authority to represent your product to a customer. Therefore, he should follow the same policy of strict honesty that you would follow yourself and should know enough about your products to represent them correctly. While you might never realize it, you will also be making many contracts each week when you write orders. Each order, when accepted, legally becomes a contract. The purchaser's order is an offer to buy. Until you have accepted it, it binds neither the purchaser nor you. Once accepted, both of you are bound by it: the customer to purchase, and you to deliver the goods.

As a matter of courtesy every order given to you should be acknowledged quickly with a postal card or letter. In practice most firms will send out a form of acknowledgment, as a card. Such a card might read: "We are pleased to receive your order *#123 of date*. We expect to ship your merchandise on or about *date*." Actually, if you start filling the customer's order within a reasonable period of time, that constitutes acceptance of that order. As a contract, an accepted order binds both parties. Your customer is obliged to buy and you are bound to ship. As a practical matter, it is questionable whether you will refuse to accept a cancellation of an order at some later date and risk incurring the customer's displeasure as well as being faced with a collection action to get your money.

However, you have the legal right to insist that he accept the goods. Conversely, if you have promised delivery by a certain date and do not deliver, your customer may suffer a loss as a result and look to you for restitution of that loss. For example, a building was scheduled to open on a given date. The supplier of furnituer could not deliver on time as agreed. His customer had to rent furniture, and the cost of rental was legitimately charged to the supplier as a result of his failure to deliver.

Sales taxes are another obligation that you will incur by the very act of selling, if a sales tax applies in your area. It would be well for you to query your accountant on your liability for such taxes, or in the absence of an accountant who is knowledgeable in these matters, to inquire of your city and state tax departments as to what taxes you must pay.

In New York, for example, a wholesaler shipping to retailers is not obliged to collect sales tax, but he must show the resale number of the purchaser in his records. Such matters are simply disposed of if provided for at the beginning of a business operation. If they are allowed to slide, you can find yourself with an impatient tax collector pressing you for monies which have not been included in your price.

A couple of other common legal misconceptions have often given inexperienced entrepreneurs some uneasy moments. One misconception is that once an object is marked with a price, or a price is published in a catalog, you are obliged to sell at that price. If you have made a mistake of this kind, and it is minor, it is perhaps better to live with it and not to raise any question. However, if you have marked a piece X $12.00 and it should be $1,200, don't believe that you have to sell it for $12.00. A transaction is binding only when an offer is made *and accepted*. The customer can offer you $12.00 for the piece, but you are not bound until you have accepted the offer.

Similarly, the idea is widely held among merchants that you cannot refuse to sell to anyone who wants to buy. You can select your customers. As a wholesaler, sensible merchandising policy demands that you do so to protect your image. While the law prevents you from discriminating against a customer because of color, religion, or nationality, you can decide that you do not wish to sell a customer for other valid reasons and simply refuse to do so.

To cover every legal eventuality a young business might encounter would require a business law library and years of study. In day to day business most people do not think about lawyers or lawsuits, and you, as a businessman, should not be overly concerned with the legal implications of your round of daily work. Lee Epstein stated his view that it is the lawyer's function to prevent litigation where possible and went on to say that the new craftsman-merchant probably should not retain an attorney except for specific matters such as drawing up incorporation papers. He did suggest, however, that buying an hour of a reputable attorney's time just to discuss the new business and seek his practical advice might be a good investment. He noted that, since most attorneys will charge their clients with a view to what the client can pay, an hour of professional advice and discussion might cost in the neighborhood of $30.00.

In practice, it is frequently difficult to say where an accountant's services end and where the attorney's begin, and also, how an intelligent minimum business insurance program will cover business risks. Generally speaking, if the lawyer's services can be overlooked or minimized at the start, the services of an accountant and a good insurance broker should not be put off. A good bookkeeping system and minimal protection can prevent a good deal of energy being expended on worrying that might better, and more enjoyably, be spent in doing what you set out to do: making and selling your things.

# Appendix

## BUYING OFFICES

In very rare instances only do buying offices actually buy esoteric merchandise for their member stores. The resident buyers of these offices have the job of seeking out new merchandise and making it known to the buyers of their member stores through mailings, news bulletins, and periodic meetings. In the main, the member stores serviced by the offices listed below are department stores.

The buying office can help you in several ways. A communication to the resident buyer will give you the names of member stores in their group and a special request to the buying offices, if you describe your product clearly, should bring an answer telling you which store buyers to contact in selling your product. When you have had a successful sales experience with one store in the group—i.e., the store bought it and resold it well—you should advise the resident buyer of the department and group in which you sold. His report of your success to other group stores can result in business for you.

There are literally hundreds of generalized and specialized buying services in the U.S.A. They serve both U.S. and foreign clients. A list of some of the principal offices which might be helpful to the craftsman-in-production follows:

Allied Purchasing Corporation
401 Fifth Avenue
New York, N.Y. 10016

Arkwright, Inc.
50 West 44th Street
New York, N.Y. 10018

Associated Merchandising Corporation
1440 Broadway
New York, N.Y. 10018

Associated Dry Goods Corporation
417 Fifth Avenue
New York, N.Y. 10016

Frederick Atkins, Inc.
11 West 42nd Street
New York, N.Y. 10036

Gimbels Corporate Buying Office
116 West 32nd Street
New York, N.Y. 10001

Independent Retailers Syndicate
33 West 34th Street
New York, N.Y. 10001

Kirby, Block & Company, Inc.
393 Seventh Avenue
New York, N.Y. 10001

Macy's Corporate Buying Division
151 West 34th Street
New York, N.Y. 10001

May Department Store Company
50 West 44th Street
New York, N.Y. 10036

119

McGreevey, Werring & Howell
225 West 34th Street
New York, N.Y. 10001

Mutual Buying Syndicate
11 West 42nd Street
New York, N.Y. 10036

Specialty Stores Association
1441 Broadway
New York, N.Y. 10018

# WHOLESALE AND TRADE PUBLICATIONS OF POSSIBLE INTEREST TO CRAFTSMEN

The personnel of trade publications are in constant touch with their own, specialized markets. They are, for that reason, often valuable sources of current information regarding trade practices and marketing guidance. A subscription to those trade publications covering markets of interest to you should be one of your early, small investments. In addition, such books can often provide you with information on the following:

1. dates and locations of trade shows and sales conventions,

2. publishers and availability of trade directories,

3. leads to distributors and outlets in the trade.

The publications of interest to you, specifically, will depend on the nature of your particular products. Some of the most important to the craftsman are:

Architectural Forum
Time & Life Building
50th Street & Sixth Avenue
New York, N.Y.

Architectural Record
330 West 42nd Street
New York, N.Y.

Arts and Architecture
3305 Wilshire Blvd.
Los Angeles, California

College Store Journal
National Association of College
   Stores Inc.
55 East College Street
Oberlin, Ohio

Contract
6118 North Sheridan Rd.
Chicago 26, Ill.
      also
7 East 43rd Street
New York, N.Y.

Display World
407 Gilbert Avenue
Cincinnati, Ohio
      also
246 Fifth Avenue
New York, N.Y.

Floor Covering Weekly
350 Fifth Avenue
New York, N.Y.

Footwear News
7 East 12th Street
New York, N.Y.

Gifts & Decorative Accessories
212 Fifth Avenue
New York 10, N.Y.

Gift & Tableware Reporter
111 Fourth Avenue
New York, N.Y.

Handbags & Accessories
111 Fourth Avenue
New York, N.Y.

Hats Magazine
152 West 42nd Street
New York, N.Y.

Home Furnishings Daily
7 East 12th Street
New York, N.Y.

Housewares Buyer
122 East 42nd Street
New York, N.Y.

Housewares Review
111 Fourth Avenue
New York, N.Y.

Institutions
1801 Prairie Avenue
Chicago, Ill.

Interior Decorator's News
11 West 42nd Street
New York 18, N.Y.

Interior Design
151 East 50th Street
New York 22, N.Y.
        also
4 East Ohio
Chicago, Ill.

Interiors
18 East 50th Street
New York 22, N.Y.

Lamp Journal
101 Springfield Avenue
Summit, N.J.

Lighting
2 West 45th Street
New York, N.Y.

Linens & Domestics
25 West 45th Street
New York, N.Y.

Progressive Architecture
430 Park Avenue
New York, N.Y. 10022

Toys and Novelties
111 Fourth Avenue
New York, N.Y.

Upholstering Magazine
230 Fifth Avenue
New York 1, N.Y.

Wallpaper & Wallcoverings
114 East 32nd Street
New York 16, N.Y.

Women's Wear Daily
7 East 12th Street
New York 3, N.Y.

# PERMANENT NATIONAL MARKET CENTERS

The following are key wholesale market centers of special interest to craftsmen. While many local centers exist, and other centers exist for specific trades, the following are of general national importance. At these centers, principal regional and national wholesale representatives often have showrooms for selling to their trades. As a "manufacturer," you will be admitted to most of them. All have information centers and most will furnish a directory of their tenants upon request. They can be especially helpful in assisting you to get a concentrated picture of the trades in which you are selling and in locating sales representatives.

## California

The Brack Shops
527 West 7th Street
Los Angeles

Merchandise Mart
712 South Olive Street
Los Angeles

Western Merchandise Mart
240 Peachtree Street
San Francisco

Los Angeles Homefurnishings Mart
1933 South Broadway
Los Angeles

## Georgia

Atlanta Merchandise Mart
240 Peachtree St., N.W.
Atlanta

## Illinois

The Merchandise Mart
Chicago 54

## New York

Gift & Art Center
225 Fifth Avenue

## Texas

The Dallas Trade Mart
2300 Stemmons Freeway
Dallas

# Index